We met a[t] ...
in Liberty ... es

Love Yourself:
The Second Great Commandment Part B

By
Raymond Burks, Sr.

Love Yourself
The Second Great Commandment Part B
by Raymond Burks, Sr

Printed in the United States of America

ISBN 9781613796986

Unless otherwise indicated, Bible quotations are taken from The King James Version.

www.xulonpress.com

Dedication

To the many Bible class teachers, ministers and pastors that poured spiritual wealth into my life, by motivating me to be a student of Christian discipleship. Thank you.

To all that are in circumstances that requires self-love adjustment.

Acknowledgements

Thank God for the inspiration and the insight to pen this teaching. Without Him there is no love.

I wish to thank my wife, Maria, for her patience and understanding during my time of study and writing.

This effort is a product of many whose input and perspective have provided help to generate the knowledge I placed in this book.

I wish to especially acknowledge the efforts of Dr. Diane Reid for her support.

Table of Contents

Chapter One

Introduction

This writing is motivated by the scripture text where Jesus Christ was tempted to define the most important of the Mosaic Law. His response declared it paramount that we must sincerely love our God with all that we have inside of us. And then He immediately followed that declaration with the command that we love our neighbors as ourselves. He indicated that all of the Mosaic Law was founded on these two laws or concepts. We have chosen to focus on the Second Great Commandment because it requires an enormous amount of study about ourselves and utilizes the results of that study to enhance our relationship with the rest of the world. I indicate the rest of the world because there are only two categories of people on the planet; your neighbors and your enemies. Or, you could restate the categories as the people that are your supporters, well wishers, people who mean you no harm and those who find you insignificant but are not against you – your neighbors. The next set involves those who find no reason to support you, dislike you or have reason to be your adversary – your enemies, who are your neighbors also. Despite their position relative to you, they share the planet with you and must be addressed in some manner or eventually given some thought.

The scriptures insist that we love our neighbors as we love ourselves. This implies that we already know how to love ourselves. We may have some form of selfishness akin to love of ourselves, but normally we have little or no idea of how to love ourselves without some training or some example of this characteristic. God built into our being a certain fondness for affection that remains active throughout our lives. As we learn to nurture that fondness for affection, we are then able to display to others what we have learned to require. The typical person has had no formal lessons on how to love themselves so the model is usually to follow the example of those with whom we have been involved. Our built-in mimicking system causes us to develop an understanding based on the examples that we observe. We don't even get the opportunity to choose the initial person or persons after whom we model ourselves. Whoever resides in closest proximity to us gets the grand role of mentor by default. This often means that we adapt the behavior of others who may have behaved in such a way to only benefit their personal needs, desires, and/or pleasures but not necessarily the Biblical command. No matter how you best learn, you will adapt to the normal routine behavior of those with whom you are exposed. You will naturally assume that the activity that you see is to be accepted as love of one's self. If your examples appear to be pleased or happy with the way things are going, you will find no reason to alter that model. Consequently, you could have been abused and because the person performing the abuse enjoyed abusing you, they imply that it's alright, making you think that it's right. This obviously means that most of us define what we desire as love based on the opinions of others. When others compliment a feature of our character we begin to think that it's right to maximize that trait, and in doing so, we begin to feel good about ourselves and our abilities. Despite this encouragement to emphasize our success, this does not constitute our own love for ourselves.

Unaware of ourselves, we find that when we feed our weakest character flaw, we can develop affection for the things that stroke that flaw. For example, when we discover that feeding our mouth with something that tastes good distracts us from bad feelings and deters thoughts about our problems, we find solace in eating. We may hate the effects of consuming but enjoy everything else about it. Our bodies will attempt to inform us of overindulgence, known as a form of self-preservation, but the good feeling can force us to ignore it. Such indulgence can make us forget that self preservation is an important part of loving ourselves. We may not be aware of the self-protection mechanisms that God has installed in our bodies, so some of us consider self-preservation a part of loving ourself. So it is necessary to define loving one's self so that the rest of the teaching will make sense.

Loving yourself involves taking care of the things that will cause the best end result for you. Those things may be distasteful or painful at the time of enactment but will eventually benefit you in some manner. Satisfying your internal lusts, greed or pity does not imply that you have any love for yourself. The instantaneous gratification may in fact be harmful to you and develop into a conclusion that you did not care for yourself at all. When you love yourself today, five years from now you will know that you did all of the right things for yourself, to benefit yourself with respect, and to live with yourself in dignity. Such awesome responsibility will require self-sacrifice, self-denial and extreme commitment to self in order to benefit yourself. This level of effort is real work, but it pays off in the long run. We will do an extensive study on how you can love you without being selfish. Moderation is a key detail in addressing the concept of love for yourself. We will investigate how respecting yourself fits into the concept of loving yourself. We will also investigate how self-denial can sometimes be the greatest expression of love for yourself.

One factor must be considered as you observe these concepts; you were designed by a deity greater than you and with purpose. To deny such would mean that these writings are of no meaningful benefit to you and can only be entertaining and thought provoking. The psalmist, David, wrote in **Psalms 53:1 The fool hath said in his heart, *There is no God. Corrupt are they, and have done abominable iniquity: *there is* none that doeth good.** It is not my quest to assign validity to your faith association, but this writing is directed at those who claim to be believers. Thus, these writings are motivated by inspiration of the Holy Spirit and not by secular logic. As we proceed through these teachings you will begin to see that knowing how to love yourself can help you to understand loving someone else. It will also help you to understand when you are in a relationship with someone else who really doesn't love you. You will define how you want to be loved.

Our theme scripture is from the gospel of Mark in the Holy Bible.

Mark 12:29 And Jesus answered him, The first of all the commandments is, Hear, O Israel; The Lord our God is one Lord: 30 And thou shalt love the Lord thy God with all thy heart, and with all thy soul, and with all thy mind, and with all thy strength: this is the first commandment. 31 And the second is like, namely this, Thou shalt love thy neighbour as thyself. There is none other commandment greater than these.

The odd implied concept here is if you treat others the way you want to be treated; only the best can ever happen to those in your circle of influence. By circle of influence, I mean your neighbors. The effort involved here really means that you would think before you act or speak, think about what you might say, and be careful of the emotions of others. It also means that you afford others the same behavior, respect, and opportunity as you would desire for yourself. It is a tall order when most don't really try to apply the concept of love to themselves, sincerely.

Conceptual Summary

1. The Holy Bible, containing the Mosaic Law, is the foundation for developing the behavior for, internal emotions associated with, and the comprehension of desired human treatment.

2. Most of the conscious expectations are based on what was commanded and what we desire for ourselves.

3. Outside entities influence these expectations because we allow them to and even give those influences the power to determine internal emotions.

4. Knowing what is best for ourselves is a characteristic often unavailable to us because of those exterior influences.

5. God is an influence that is necessary to acknowledge in this quest to understand how to love self.

6. The act of loving self requires conscious thought and purposeful effort.

7. We must be willing to address our individual approach to what is required for love then implement that love for self and to self.

Thought Provoking Queries

1. Is my effort to have affection for myself important enough to continue with this reading?

2. Do I have any concept of how to love myself?

3. Do I practice the behavior of loving myself enough to know how to apply that practice to others?

4. Is my purpose for loving myself to improve my relationship with others?

5. Am I morally concerned about my behavior enough to care how I treat others?

Chapter Two

What Do I Consider to Be Love of Me?

B efore you can impose your love of yourself on others, you must determine if you love yourself, how you love yourself, and if there are limitations on that expression. This requires an extensive look at whom you think you are and your personal standards of affectionate treatment. You must believe that you know who you are before starting this process. So you may have to ask yourself questions about situations and circumstances that you may find to be uncomfortable to even think. Part of this process is eliminating the noise of outside influence; this deals with what you think and not the opinions of others. Developing an opinion of yourself about your characteristics, skills and feelings will only assist you in understanding why you treat yourself in certain manners. When you look at this without the bias of outside influence, you may be baffled, but the result will be independent of what others may think.

Public opinion has value because you give it value. The person who values their own independent thinking most will make the opinions of others fodder for consideration only. To show you how important it is to isolate this process imagine the influences that can occur. If you think that having someone identify you as a dog is their show of love for you, both of you may have some level of disrespect for you. Despite the fact that dogs, as pets, are given elevated status by pet owners, their status can be different and extremely undesirable by the rest of the world. If you feel that everyone else has an advantage over you because of some character flaw, consider that you don't understand the principles of God's love and mercy. If you are struggling with the fact that you were the first child, middle child, or last child and that knowledge comes with some disadvantage, you may not know how to love. For this exercise you are allowing the opinions of others to have too much influence over a critical process in your life. Public opinion may be vital to other processes, opportunities for achievement and even judgment, but for determining how you feel about yourself, they have no place. They can provide instantaneous gratification, sense of esteem and spotlight notoriety, but because of its nature that opinion only leaves you grasping for more.

We typically acknowledge the display of love as the behavior that we have seen others perform and identify as their affection to another. This makes it important that a child has the presence of both mother and father (or someone fulfilling those roles) as they are maturing. Hopefully they will at some point observe seasons of affection, compassionate care, and commitment from that union. The lack of completeness in this picture should not have a direct impact on how you feel about yourself, although many use it as a gauge to determine future relationships. The problem, with using parents as a gauge in which to measure affection in relationships, is most parents hide their moments of affection from their children. So all the children see is the occasional flashes of affection often in spite of seasons of crisis, which is hardly an example of how love is displayed. This leads to an assumption of love without tangible evidence. If, by chance, the parents put on a display of affection for more than a flash, the children can sometimes deduct that the parents are ignoring them. In essence, the paradox remains that having parents around to give love to the individual child does not necessarily give the child a picture of how love should be received or what it means to be or feel loved.

If you think that restricting or limiting the best in life from yourself is love because of the concept that extravagance is overkill, you may have some issues with self-esteem. Extravagance in the face of despair may appear untimely and selfish, but denial of good things for yourself does not indicate that you love yourself or anyone else. Often selfishness defined is equated to self love over-done. Unfortunately, self-denial does not necessarily indicate a balance or even understanding how to love one's self either. There must be an evaluation of personal requirement, moderation, and the availability of accommodation. After the evaluation, judgment of the circumstances will help determine whether restricting or limiting is necessary, however, how you treat yourself does not accurately depict how you feel about yourself.

Since we have little of your history to base any assessment on, we must accept your personal evaluation of how you feel. Only you know how much you do or don't love yourself. As a condition of this text we ask that you make a conscious decision to learn who you really are in order that you learn to love yourself. There are questions that you must consider in detail concerning who you are that will assist you in this exercise. That internal knowledge will help you to understand the inner person, make determinations based on that understanding, and eventually live with the results of those actions. You will later find out that this does not necessarily mean pampering yourself to oblivion, or ensuring that you are denied no luxury, or even that you demand that everyone you meet give you the utmost honor and respect. But it does indicate that you exercise all of them with some level of moderation. You will mature in the act of loving yourself.

So the model that we hope to ultimately apply is the one that Jesus Christ lived, but before we elevate to that lofty level of spirituality, let us start here on earth. We all remember the affection and care that our mothers gave us in our early years. This was defined as a mother's love. Many of us enjoyed it so much that we refused to give mother a rest as long as she has lived. That love involved being a provider, even though we never knew where she got the things that she provided. That love involved being a teacher; her knowledge was supreme although we later learned that she wasn't exactly the smartest person on the planet. That love involved some level of self-sacrifice which we may not have appreciated at the time that we received the benefit of it. That love involved our mother being a living example of affection heavily sprinkled with misunderstanding on our part. **Proverb 22:6 Train up a child in the way he should go: and when he is old, he will not depart from it.** That love involved some correction even though sometimes we perceived that mother was wrong. And that love involved compassion to ease the pains, loneliness, and misunderstandings. If you are an adult now, you will have to replace all of the "love" that momma gave with some of your own.

The responsibility that you have is to do so without taxing the efforts of someone who is not you.

If you had your father around, the love he most likely provided involved teaching you that at some point you had to respect him – he didn't necessarily give you respect but he expected it from you. His love involved helping you to understand your limitations without the loss of your confidence in your abilities. He should have also provided a sense of security, stability and reliance as his show of love to you and the family. And if you are an adult, these are additional traits that must be somehow added to your inventory of love characteristics. **Colossians 3:20 Children, obey your parents in all things: for this is well pleasing unto the Lord. 21 Fathers, provoke not your children to anger, lest they be discouraged.** As you can see, fathers often could be so callused in their approach to children that their behavior could cause discontentment. However, strength of character, discipline, and persistence are qualities that will assist you in loving yourself also.

Many will use the lack of parental presence as an excuse to indicate deficiency. They tend to observe that others had something that they did not, and that it was a strong contributor to their character. Despite the lack of the physical presence of a mother and/or a father, often the roles are filled by others in the community. Other people in your life can fill a substitute role for you, sometimes providing a better example than you may have received from the real parents. Hope and love is where you find it. For the majority, someone will be there to fulfill the duties of a mother and father; however awareness of the lack will impact your perspective going forward. For the sake of our study, the missing parent or parents will not change the potential outcome. You will still have some foundation for maturing the 'love yourself' behavior.

As you get older, you learn about love provided by the community, friends, associates, and co-workers. Often this circle of influence provides avenues of communication that you may feel are more substantial than those at home because these people are in your age group. Typically, they speak your language, enjoy your circumstances, and live the ideal lifestyle as defined by public opinion. They don't have experience but they are experiencing at the same time as you are; apparently a misery loves company thing. Unfortunately, they are often more responsible for shaping your opinion of yourself than anyone else. They don't necessarily deserve that right but you probably gave it to them without knowing it. This is the typical model that most of the modern world and society uses as the paradigm that shapes their personal self-worth, ego, and love of themselves. If it all turns out good, you are blessed. If it turns out somewhat negative you need some adjustments in your life because you really have no idea how to love someone else if you haven't been loved.

Let's go deeper; from life's observations we have assessed that the children that received everything that they ask for have often accused their parents of not loving them. Physical trophies, gifts, and possessions are obtained at a cost that deprives children of their parents' time and causes the children to wish that they had what they don't have. So it seems that having all of life's trinkets doesn't translate into being loved, nor does it imply that you love yourself.

Trinkets or not, when they are removed from your inventory, you still must deal with internal feelings. Meanwhile children who have had little have implied that their families were full of love. So wealth and possessions do not necessarily define how a person feels about being loved, neither does the lack of wealth and possessions. A constant flow of information has its comfort, but communication does not always indicate that the communication link is a sign of love. When you consider all of the tangibles that can contribute to the expression of love, only the perception of being loved matters. It is an individual choice to perceive that someone really cares for you. You have no tangible evidence that your perception is true other than how you feel. People may do things for you for a variety of reasons such as: they feel a sense of obligation, it's the proper thing to do, or it is the expectation that must be fulfilled in order to maintain peace. None of those actions necessarily involve love. Furthermore, what others do for you has no bearing on what you feel inside about yourself.

Then there are other types of contributors to how much we love ourselves and what value we place on our self-worth. It is those significant incidents that occur in our lives that cause us to devalue, belittle, blame, sometimes feel extremely proud, label ourselves and separate ourselves from humanity. Those incidents may be significant to you while they are being totally ignored by those who may have been involved in the same incidents at the time. These character shaping events can be remembered indefinitely or forgotten on the surface impacting your behavior and feelings for life. Some of those character shaping incidents include creating victims of abuse, scorn, hurt and humiliation which often leave scars that apparently never heal. It leaves a mark that demands an answer that often is unobtainable. As the demand for that answer grows in magnitude, it has the potential to cause more behavioral patterns to develop in shaping who you are and how you feel about yourself. There are those who won their high school sporting event which they allowed to define to themselves who they are. They milk that fifteen minutes of fame until it is drained completely dry, and then they spend the remainder of their life looking for a replacement fifteen minutes of fame. You may not have even been involved in the events personally, but they may have impacted your belief system. For example, if your father was a quarterback in his youth, you might believe that you should be athletic too; only to find that you don't fit the mold. With that information you make comparisons that cause you to wonder about your place in life and about loving yourself. Events and circumstances often influence us but are not suppose to define us. If you allow events and circumstances to define who you are, they graduate into elements of your affection for yourself.

So when you take all of this into consideration you may find that the person that you see in the mirror each day is not the person that you wish to be. There may be a lot to overcome, but it is paramount that you love yourself better so that you can understand how to love your neighbor. It is suggested that you take a few minutes to evaluate how you feel about yourself, but you probably already know.

With all of the outside influences impacting your opinion, you may not have an opinion of what you think loving yourself is. In some cases, you may have a definite understanding of what love is not for you. However, the reverse of what love is not does not necessarily fit into the mold of what love is. If you are certain that taking verbal abuse daily is not love, it is not reasonable to believe that flattery is love. Unfortunately, flattery usually comes with purpose. If you believe that your parents punished you too much and that is not real love in your eyes, zero punishment does not constitute love either. So you must eliminate the noise, and define the substance of what you personally believe that love is for you and to you. Then you must determine what qualifies as enacting love upon yourself.

Meanwhile we often accept that whatever type of emotional contact we receive from others to be classified as love. This is really wrong; it explains why many relationships go awry. The replacement affection is often something less than desirable unless desperation is the motivator. Just any 'ole' love is not the cure for what ails you. Abusive affection is not love. Love by exception is not satisfactory or a replacement for the love you will learn about as you study. An after-thought of affection is not the love that you need. The affection that you get because everyone else is gone or because the favorites didn't want what was offered is not acceptable. Sex is not love. There are many things that are accepted in the place of love that have nothing to do with love. Suitable substitutes for affection are only a perception of fulfillment.

So what is this love that I really need? I need affection that is not conditional and is without strings attached. I need love that is reliable despite my inability to return the same level of commitment. I need love that is not defined by how I look, how smart I am, whom I know, where I've been or who is my friend. I need love that will be cognizant of my needs, my desires, and my opinion. It becomes quite obvious that rarely will we find such commitment in a human being, but if we learn how to love ourselves, we can make an attempt to provide that kind of love to others. It becomes apparent that if God is the essence of love, then I must learn about this special gift from Him. His technical manual describes love unmerited, love despite anger, love of the unlovable and love of the deficient. God expected me to study Him so that I could become better at loving myself.

When I define what love is to me, I have to consider that I am responsible to execute and exercise all available knowledge to support my existence today and going forward. That is compounded by the fact that some things that I do to myself for the benefit of self-love will not necessarily feel good, support my need for gratification, immediately fulfill my desires, or bring on accolades from observers. Because no one else understands my purpose and objectives, I may have to forgo being understood in order to be at peace with myself later on in life. And as I go through this metamorphosis of learning, I must learn to gracefully accept praise and criticism equally with the skill to apply those things that I feel will benefit and ignore those things designed specifically to harm my character. The job of loving me is full-time and I am the only quality control inspector of my life until judgment day.

Conceptual Summary

1. You can determine who you are without using the bias of peer pressure, traditional rituals, or comparisons to other personalities. It is a thought-provoking exercise if you are accustomed to living to please

others while ignoring your personal needs and may require extreme discipline.

2. Should you allow the opinions of others to shape your behavior and belief system you will be enslaved to them and will lose your power to dictate your own direction.

3. Despite outside influence, you do have your own value system. You can use that value system to determine what you believe is the love that you require of yourself and of others. To do so you must eliminate behaviors aimed at yourself or conducted by you that has no long-term benefit.

4. There are people in your life that have been your role models whether they assumed the role consciously or unknowingly. Without judging, privately evaluate their contributions to you. Notice how your behavior mirrors theirs; purge the bad behaviors and mimic the good.

5. Even the loner has been involved in relationships throughout their life. Examine your feelings about your part in those relationships. Determine whether your role was of mutual benefit.

6. The spoiled child (one that has been afforded everything) has no advantage in understanding how to love themself over the deprived child (one that has been afforded little). They each must take into consideration their situations and make an evaluation of self-worth and love of self.

7. When real love is not present in one's life, any physical or emotional contact can be substituted for the missing affection. This substituted contact should be completely evaluated as part of the process of trying to understand how you feel about yourself.

8. To really understand love, one must figure out a method of displaying affection for themself that is not contingent upon how they look, how they perform, who appreciates what they offer or their achievements.

Thought Provoking Queries

1. What must I do to exclude the opinions of others from my evaluation process?

2. What are the characteristics within me that I feel define me and are those things worthy of such lofty labels?

3. If I remove those characteristics that define me will I still have value to myself? For example if I think that I have beauty, will I still have value if I am in a automobile accident and somehow lose that beauty?

4. Have I allowed the opinions of others to dictate to me who I am? If so, what happens if they leave?

5. When do I start loving me for whom I think I am?

Chapter Three

Before I Look at Others

Before we look at the opinion and evaluation that others have made of us, let us evaluate ourselves. Verify that you do like yourself. Verify what you think makes you a beautiful person to yourself. Consider how that like equates to loving yourself. For those of you who instantly determined that you really like yourself and thus love yourself, hallelujah! Meanwhile the rest of us must determine how we got to where we are now. The joyous lifestyle events and the wounding often start when we are the most impressionable. There are those incidents that happened in your youth that you allow to continue to shape your feelings about yourself and even your behavior. Despite their impact then it is time to be your age now. Living in the past excludes valuable time in your present and future. Maturing and being your age does not fix the heart or improve your perception of yourself; that takes some work. The good things that occur provide pleasant memories to ponder while everything else must be dealt with in some manner. The incident is there, the hurt remains and we really want some answers. Much of our pain comes from wanting to assign blame. We assume that if someone can take the blame then the issue can be resolved. We further assume that if we can assign the blame to someone else, at least a portion of the hurt will be shifted off of us. However, healing does not come from knowing who was at fault; healing comes from the attitude of forgiveness. Imagine if you will that Jesus required a subject to take the blame for dying on Calvary. Billions of souls would be walking around in guilt and shame. But Jesus took the guilt, shame, and blame with Him to the cross so that we could have peace, joy and rest. It would be somewhat simple if we only had others to blame but many times we blame ourselves or we choose not to forgive ourselves. Despite the fact that you were there to be the victim, you have no right or claim to be a motivator to the hurt. The condition of a person's heart determines whether they will sin or hurt others; external motivators are secondary. So take yourself out of the predator's problem because you create enough problems for yourself. Let him or her bear their own cross; you have one already. Carrying two crosses means that you have little time to love yourself.

Sometimes there are things that we do that cause us to dislike or not to love ourselves. When we make a bad choice we can feel guilt or shame for that unwise decision. We probably would get over it if it had not been such a long lasting and impacting kind of decision. We find ourselves second guessing every decision after that. It also makes us speculate about what could have happened if we would have done something different. We can get lost in wonderment and guessing. And as we observe the myriad of possibilities, we become bitter with ourselves. If I had invested in Xerox, if I had married someone else, if I had not married at all, if I had saved my money, if I had gone to college; you could speculate all day and never know what the real conclusion is. You have no control over what has already passed. You cannot change one minute of the past. It is your history and it is documented in your mind. Your efforts to worry about it won't make it better or worse. Worrying about it won't make you a better person, but it can make you have a worse attitude and make you tend to dislike or hate yourself. Lots of situations fall into this category; things that you did, things that you didn't, tangibles that you hoped for and lots of things that was or is out of reach. Never mind all of that. If it is in your past, figure out a way to come to grips with the situation and circumstance and move beyond it. If you must have closure; define what was beyond your control and eliminate those worries from your list of concerns. If it was within your power to do something about it and you didn't, accept the responsibility and decide what you will do about it now. If you messed things up and it appears that they cannot be repaired, give it to the one who has the power to fix everything. But remember that standing around talking about how bad things are does not resolve the problem. It just makes the problem last longer and grow bigger. If you are not going to work on the problem, take it off the list of things to do. You have other problems to address – get to them. Procrastination is not your friend. It merely makes you appear to be lazy and unconcerned. If you can just address the internal issues that you have you will progress towards loving yourself.

That was a large amount of information to cover about yourself. However, you won't get through that exercise if you are not honest with yourself. Lying to others can be justifiable in your mind but lying to yourself is wasted effort, because you know when you lied to yourself. And there is noone around to support the lie that you told yourself. There is no one around to argue about the pros and cons, the positives and the negatives or the points for and the points against. You are stuck with whatever assessment you make. Your justification of the lie really makes you look unwise to yourself, because you happen to know the truth. If you lie to yourself, you will lie to God. If you practice lying to yourself, you will soon begin to believe your own lies to yourself. And when you catch yourself in a lie, to whom do you get angry? Never mind; lying to yourself will make you hate yourself. You typically only get caught up in lying to yourself when you try to care more about the feelings and opinions of others than the truth. **Proverbs 26: 27 Whoso diggeth a pit shall fall therein:**

and he that rolleth a stone, it will return upon him. 28 A lying tongue hateth those that are afflicted by it; and a flattering mouth worketh ruin. So you become a hypocrite and a character or environment actor. A character actor portrays a role to fit circumstance. An environment actor performs to suit the environment or climate in which they live. The role playing always comes back to haunt you and presents situations that you will have to explain; then you have to remember to whom you told what lie. The worst of lying to yourself is that you can hide the truth from others for a long time, but the truth is just beneath the lie and you know it. Being honest and speaking the truth to yourself about yourself can be painful, but it heals and has little other consequence. It helps you to see the limitations, shortcomings and flaws, but it also gives you a starting point for resolution and closure. And the Bible says that the truth will set you free. Bondage, confinement and restraint can make you learn to love your slave-master and hate yourself. So while you are looking at yourself in the mirrors, take off the façade, remove the front, and wash away the make-up of life. The person that you see will not be the clone of your favorite movie star; the picture won't be a display of perfection that you love to watch on the nighttime soap, or the mentor that you have idolized. What you see is what you get; the plain and simple you. Once you see the real thing you can begin to work.

Before you look at others, listen to others and allow others to influence you, identify the traits about yourself that you think make you who you are. Before you allow others to tell you who you are, try to know it first. If someone else discovers something about you that you didn't know, it can be upsetting. It means that you didn't pay attention to the whole you. There is something about not understanding yourself that causes confusion. When you don't know why you did what you did, you become disappointed with yourself, and you look for someone to blame for your misunderstanding. Furthermore, when you miss the information, you have to find out where it's been hiding. All of the excuses that you might dream up have little value because there is no real supporting evidence for the excuse. You want to know why you dislike certain types of people. You want to know why certain words just get under your skin. Believe it or not, King Solomon has written a lot of scripture that describes your feelings and behavior.

Next we need to evaluate how you look at yourself in another way. It is easy to admire others when they are successful, proficient, good looking or seem to have a certain charisma. Admiring them is one thing; comparing yourself to them is another. We like to try to measure up to the standard that is set by others, using them as an excuse for not getting involved or participating. The only person that you should measure yourself against or compare yourself to is Jesus Christ. All others are merely predetermined quality standards for failure. The other reason for not measuring yourself against others is God didn't make you to be them. If He had wanted two of them He would have made twins.

Conceptual Summary

1. Before you can objectively evaluate, it is wise to gather all of the available information about whatever you are assessing. When it comes to evaluating yourself without the benefit of outside

opinion, you must honestly observe the object in the mirror.

2. When memory is the source of information, you may find that you will have to ask yourself questions that probe into areas of your being that produce painful results. You may have to accept or relinquish responsibility for events, actions and behaviors that apparently shaped your character before you can make a determination about yourself.

3. Being impressionable is not a fault or a curse. Most everyone is impressionable at one time in their life. You will often have little or no control over who is influencing your personality or character. Know that it happens, and you may not be responsible for it. Others whom may have ulterior motives and agenda may be using you to achieve their own personal goals.

4. Knowing the origin of your suffering, who implemented it on you and whatever motivated the action or behavior is simply information that is nice to

know. It really will not change the magnitude of pain or suffering.

5. Sharing the perpetrator's guilt is not a part of being the victim, and the victim has no right to being the motivator for any inflicted suffering.

6. Major character shaping and lasting pain occurs during the period in our lives when we are most impressionable. We tend to build our defense mechanisms or our security blankets based on those events.

7. Assigning blame does not displace the hurt, remove the guilt, or assist in the forgiveness process. Responsibility for activity can often be assigned with specific justification; however, the victim of the activity will remain hurt.

8. If you are the victim, you have no right to claim part in the motivation for the hurt. For example, provocative appearance may have had nothing to do with the imposed abuse. Thus the victim would have been abused despite their appearance.

9. Accepting responsibility for past events and behaviors that you are truly responsible for has been a contributor to closure.

10. The power to change the past would be an awesome tool for impacting the future. When you invent it call me.

11. Lying to yourself about yourself is an exercise in futility. Eventually you will have to face the truth as it really is.

12. Mimicking the appearance or behavior of others has some merit when attempting a success model of achievement. However, that is merely a duplication of your neighbor. To find out who you are, look inside for the traits that truly display your character in order to better understand loving yourself.

Thought Provoking Queries

1. Am I prepared to look into my history, legacy, and past to explore and investigate the incidents and events that really shaped my personality and character?

2. When I revisit the painful moments, will I require restitution, compensation, explanation, and/or revenge to move forward with this process? For the Christian pondering this question, remember that you will be forgiven in the same manner as you forgive. This statement includes forgiving yourself.

3. What will you do if it is not possible to investigate your circumstance to its fullest because the other parties involved are not available to support your healing process?

4. What will it take to release the hurt?

5. If I eliminate the characteristics and qualities of my influential family members, mentors, important figures, and friends, will I find anything of substance within to evaluate?

6. Should I find that I have no character of my own could I still love myself?

7. If what I find is all bad from my perspective, do I try to create a new me or work on the bad characteristics because they are the real me?

8. Have I lied to myself about who I am?

Chapter Four

So Where Do We Start?

Luke 21:19 **In your patience possess ye your souls.** One of the characteristics of love is patience. It is not in the typical vocabulary of any person when referring to themselves. Having patience with yourself is the beginning of loving yourself. You would think that some act of self-preservation would be the first characteristic to cover but actually patience should be first. It is because of impatience that we often punish ourselves, abuse ourselves, and belittle ourselves. Impatience generates frustration and disappointment. We happen to understand the consequences of our failure, flaws of character, procrastination, and oversight of things of importance, so we punish ourselves. We can feel the anguish that forces us to rush to complete and the act of speaking before we think, so these become additional causes to punish ourselves. Rather than allowing additional time for adjustment and/or maturing we tend to skip, drop, or ignore the task and proceed. Our love for ourselves should help us to understand that we should never shortchange ourselves. This often means that we must commit to doing things right for ourselves when perhaps we would cut corners in other situations. The picture of not loving self is most often painted by the mechanic who drives a vehicle that always needs a tune-up while his customers get great service. There is something special about the cliché that 'charity starts at home and then spreads abroad'. It really complements the second great commandment of love your neighbor as yourself. Not being patient with ourselves really means that we are more interested in instant solutions than problem solving. By obtaining instant resolutions, you gain the satisfaction of vanishing problems, but you lose the joy of gratification that comes from overcoming obstacles. You also lose the confidence that you would have gained from the encounter. So you have one less reason for loving yourself or that characteristic about yourself.

We must acknowledge that life happens fast but is not a menu item from a drive-through of choices or a selection from a computer program menu drop-down. Even if you insist on having life your way it still takes time to develop the anticipated results. Being in control means making choices for yourself, not necessarily commanding the mechanics. Due to the fact that you don't really control how things happen, you must fix your mind so that you are not frustrated by how long it takes. We sing about how God is in control, well, patience with yourself can help you accept that concept. **Matthew 6:25 Therefore I say unto you, Take no thought for your life, what ye shall eat, or what ye shall drink; nor yet for your body, what ye shall put on. Is not the life more than meat, and the body than raiment? 26 Behold the fowls of the air: for they sow not, neither do they reap, nor gather into barns; yet your heavenly Father feedeth them. Are ye not much better than they? 27 Which of you by taking thought can add one cubit unto his stature? 28 And why take ye thought for raiment? Consider the lilies of the field, how they grow; they toil not, neither do they spin: 29 And yet I say unto you, That even Solomon in all his**

glory was not arrayed like one of these. 30 Wherefore, if God so clothe the grass of the field, which to day is, and to morrow is cast into the oven, shall he not much more clothe you, O ye of little faith? 31 Therefore take no thought, saying, What shall we eat? or, What shall we drink? or, Wherewithal shall we be clothed? 32 (For after all these things do the Gentiles seek:) for your heavenly Father knoweth that ye have need of all these things. This scripture lets us know just how little control we really have of our own lives. You are allowed to believe that you are the captain of your own ship, but you must remember that as the ship becomes more complicated, the captain allows others to perform the additional duties of running it. Although the captain may know how he wants things to be done, he has to accept that others are doing it their way, hopefully to his standards. Again, patience becomes the tool that helps the person responsible for the ship and its direction to remain calm and ready to make decisions by being aware of the conditions around them. Despite the desire to be in control, you should realize you are merely second in command, considering that God is the one who is truly in control. **Matthew 10:30 But the very**

hairs of your head are all numbered. 31 Fear ye not therefore, ye are of more value than many sparrows. Certainly if God knows how much hair is on your head when you do not, you should be completely accepting that you are not in control. So it would be wise to be patient with your choices, decisions, and yourself. Look past the circumstances of the moment and see the better future. If the future that you see is bleak, acknowledge that now you have something to work on and pray to God.

Another advantage to being patient with yourself is that you give yourself a chance to prove to yourself that you have tolerance. Accented or emphasized good qualities do not cancel the bad qualities in a person. Despite your good qualities, you are acutely aware of the fact that you are not perfect. You may tell others about your endless pursuit of perfection, but deep in your heart you know all of your flaws. And you can be brutal to yourself concerning those flaws, especially when no one else is around to temper that criticism. You know better than anyone the consequences of your actions and how those flaws have impacted your life. You can't really talk to anyone else about them, without extreme trust, because they may use that information against you for gossip or to make themselves feel like they are superior to you. These issues follow you all of your life unless you seek divine assistance. Because God made you, only God can fix the flaws permanently. Getting help from God will either help you with the situation generated by your flaws or fix the flaw. This is something to consider when trying to love yourself. You would think that being impatient with yourself would have some advantages. But, chewing yourself out gains you nothing but more anguish. Belittling yourself because of oversight or mistakes really only makes you feel bad and doesn't address the issue. Meanwhile patience with yourself can give you hope for something better. **Romans 5:3 And not only so, but we glory in tribulations also: knowing that tribulation worketh patience; 4 And patience, experience; and experience, hope: 5 And hope maketh not ashamed;** Part of the experience of life is that we continually learn. So if we are patient with ourselves the hope is that we will get better. We will have more reason to love ourselves. As you might guess, this allows looking forward to a better you because of hope and patience. **Romans 8:25 But if**

we hope for that we see not, then do we with patience wait for it.

There are times that we destroy our hope because of our lack of patience with ourselves. It's not that we don't want the best for ourselves but our quick tongues speak away any chance of a blessing or a better future. We get discouraged and began to talk about what will not happen, what cannot occur, what bad thing is going to happen and how nothing good can happen because of certain conditions. God didn't block it and the devil didn't take it; you spoke it away because you chose to speak before you thought. **Proverb 15:3 The eyes of the LORD are in every place, beholding the evil and the good. 4 A wholesome tongue is a tree of life: but perverseness therein is a breach in the spirit.** So you can see that you can do yourself damage in what you speak. Be careful about what doubt and misdeed that you speak upon yourself. A little patience, a little hope can change the future.

Conceptual Summary

1. There is more to having patience with one's self than waiting with alleged purpose. The anticipation of results, the assignment of consequence, and the sense of completeness all contribute to personal patience.

2. Procrastination only makes the act of patience take longer and avoidance of the issues only make the suffering last.

3. Punishing yourself does not change the situation or make you feel any better about not achieving a solution. In fact, the punishment actually hurts, too.

4. If you would do a great job for another individual, you should consider doing an even greater job for yourself. It will provide you with a sense of pride in workmanship, a reminder that you can do good work, and a lasting memory of achievement.

5. Consider that God controls the total outcome and your contribution to it should be one that you would not mind reviewing in His presence.

6. It is paramount that you know your limitations, but it is depressing to glorify them. When you define your limitations the only reason to dwell on those concepts is to reduce the limitations or to correct them.

7. Take time to learn the lessons that caused you anguish; review the past sequence of events, analyze your behavior, consider what you can perform better next time to avoid repeating the same mistakes.

8. The boldness to speak a thought is the initiation of faith, whether in yourself or in God.

Thought Provoking Queries

1. Have you ever thought about taking time to analyze your behavior, qualities, and objectives? This is a process that will require serious and deep thought, but should be considered after every trial, crisis, problem, or major decision.

2. Have you considered how long it takes to justify procrastination and its' benefits? If you think that

procrastination has benefits then you must define what time period is enough wasted time.

3. If a task is not worthy of you performing it best for yourself, who is more worthy of your service other than God?

4. Are you willing to work on your shortcomings and limitations? Consider the amount of effort required to make yourself a better person.

Chapter Five

Self-Discipline for Self-Love

The next show of self-love is the exercise of self-restraint, discipline and moderation. Society considers these qualities to be strong contributors to the whole person concept, but as an individual they are required just to remain in control. They fortify the characteristics of personal ethics, respect, and positive projection in a person, which is perceived to be a display of self-love. Lack of these traits could be conceived as greed, selfishness, and wantonness. Often we find ourselves enjoying an indulgence to the point of destruction. We indulge until satisfaction is gained, and the negative affects begin to engage. This type of behavior does not display love; it only presents a picture of the lack of self-restraint or discipline. Many times your body will tell you when you have had enough of something, but because it feels good, tastes good, boosts your ego, or makes you think of yourself as superior, you find yourself continuing in that behavior. Or, the opposite example is when your body tells you that you need to exercise, take your medicine, or change your behavior but instead of listening to the need (showing love) you find an easier escape. The scriptures indicate that you should exercise moderation because you are being watched. That would more strongly indicate that your moderation is now important to you, because your love of yourself makes you want to be well respected. **Philippians 4:5 Let your moderation be known unto all men. The Lord is at hand. 6 Be careful for nothing; but in every thing by prayer and supplication with thanksgiving let your requests be made known unto God. 7 And the peace of God, which passeth all understanding, shall keep your hearts and minds through Christ Jesus.** As we deteriorate or fail to exercise moderation, we watch others maintain and we wonder how they do it. To keep yourself healthy or to love yourself, you need to force yourself to be moderate in your practices or behaviors.

This applies to the physical, mental and spiritual sides of life. If you don't work the body, the body will forget how to work. If you don't stimulate your mind, it will become stagnated in simple and routine thinking. If you don't stimulate growth in your spirit, it, too, will start to die. These things require your commitment to discipline and self-restraint. For most things, if you don't remind yourself of this commitment to yourself something will come along and challenge it. The short distance runner that dreams of running a mile, with diligence and persistence will find themselves running further than a mile because they can. Weight lifters find themselves able to lift more over time because what they were lifting previously has become light. And if you develop a desire to build up your spirit man, you will find that spiritual things will become more desirable. This principle seems to apply when considering physical and mental development, also. The need for discipline surfaces when other things distract you from loving yourself. Those who cause these distractions have a strong argument because they are defending their personal interest, which happens to have a higher priority in their circumstance than your love for yourself. In their eyes, your love of self demands second place as they feel you should be supporting their interests. To counter the deterrence to your attention to yourself, you must remember the consequences of self neglect.

The restraint to exercise moderation normally requires something stronger than your will power. Moderation must be taken seriously because some things may be acceptable under control while excessiveness could mean sin. While you are eating the cake, it's available and you already know how good it tastes. To stop eating it in the middle of the effort seems sacrilege but if eating the whole thing is going to have a negative impact on your health, your moderation and your love for yourself is required. This is normally a trait that should have been taught to you when you were a child, but in order to keep you from making endless wailing and noise your parents probably just let you have whatever it was that you didn't need – no offense to the parents. Sometimes a simple reminder can help you with this type love; other times you may require a strong motivator. But for the sake of loving yourself, do what is best for you, which should not involve feeding the greed.

Self-discipline is the one character of self-love that most want to ignore. It is required to achieve almost every facet of accomplishment. **I Corinthians 9:24 Know ye not that they which run in a race run all, but one receiveth the prize? So run, that ye may obtain. 25 And every man that striveth for the mastery is temperate in all things. Now they do it to obtain a corruptible crown; but we are incorruptible. 26 I therefore so run, not as uncertainly; so fight I, not as one that beateth the air: 27 But I keep under my body, and bring it into subjection: lest that by any means, when I have preached to others, I myself should be a castaway.** If you have a God given skill, it normally doesn't become refined or excellent until some measure of effort has been exerted to achieve that level of excellence. To get there means that you will have to exercise it, work on improvement, and evaluate the performance regularly to gain the prowess that you may desire or need to be effective. If you work at a thing long enough you will get better; there will be improvement. Basketball players who find themselves challenged at the free-throw line can alleviate the problem with practice. Implementing and maintaining the practice until it's no longer needed is the part where self-discipline is manifested. When your self-esteem has been bruised due to criticism of some physical character trait you can impose some self-love by exercising self-discipline in a number of ways that address the issue. This doesn't apply exclusively to physical issues but involves a number of things including health issues like high cholesterol, diabetes, etc. Still sometimes it takes self-discipline to achieve routine tasks because we often do not feel like doing some things for ourselves. As your quality of life suffers so will your feelings for yourself and others.

In order for self-discipline to be effective you must know what your weaknesses are without dwelling on them. In other words, don't make your weaknesses a god; they are impacting enough without you glorifying them. Also, don't use your weakness just to get attention.

Conceptual Summary

1. The expectations of good citizenship involve exercising self-discipline, self-restraint, and moderation. These qualities are major contributors to the act of

loving one's self for more reasons than acknowledged by society, healthcare or financial gurus.

2. There is a price to be paid to achieve the consequences of self-control and moderation. The achievement alone will motivate more self-acceptance than was present before the effort.

3. Overindulgence in any pleasure can lead to addiction, and the consequences will display a lack of love for one's self.

4. Watching others maintain their self-control should be a motivator for our endeavor, but we shouldn't compete with others to be ourselves. Defining ourselves by using others as a measuring stick eventually means that we become the other person instead of just improving our own character.

5. When you measure your progress against the efforts that you made, you tend to strive to be a better you.

6. If you focus on improving on the flaw that you know about in you, the outcome is an improved person that is easier to accept and to love.

Thought Provoking Queries

1. How can I determine which areas of self-control will benefit me the most?

2. Where do I need to focus self-control or self-discipline to maintain a lifestyle that promotes my longevity?

3. Can I identify the areas in my life that are suffering because of my lack of commitment to loving myself?

4. How do I define the cost that I am willing to pay to indulge myself today so I can to shift the suffering consequence to tomorrow?

5. Am I really getting value out of overindulgence today?

6. What would I lose if I gave up my vices for a better future?

Chapter Six

The Poor Me Syndrome Modified

Putting your weakness in the forefront in order to be the center of attraction gets you your fifteen minutes of fame but it also gets you a label of being weak in that area. Labels and nicknames are difficult to eliminate. It isn't wise to use your weakness to gain favor either; if you are a Christian you will have favor enough without belittling yourself. Don't allow your weaknesses to dominate your feelings. This can become a ticket to depression unless you choose to think about something else – preferably something spiritual and holy. Don't use your weaknesses as an excuse or an escape to do wrong or to get away with something. Excuses are like lies; no one benefits from them or wants to hear them except the person who tells them.

However, knowing your weaknesses keeps you abreast of where your ability ends and where God's power, will, and expectations begin. You may question God's expectations of you, but God's expectations of you are the point where your faith in Him takes hold. Spiritual growth develops as faith is exercised. And faith is exercised when you perform beyond your limitations or weaknesses. You learn more about yourself and how to deal with emotions, physical qualifications, and comprehensions. Thus, the result is knowing how to love yourself even more. Knowing your weaknesses can keep you out of trouble. If you stay away from areas where your weaknesses will be exploited you may avoid some sins. If you happen to remove just a little of the guilt that plagues life you can find reason to love yourself even more.

If you really want to show yourself love, work to turn your weaknesses into your strengths. That probably sounds like an oxymoron. However, many times you can work on a weakness and it can become your strength. If that is not your personal objective seek from on high. **Philippines 4:11 Not that I speak in respect of want:**

for I have learned, in whatsoever state I am, therewith to be content. 12 I know both how to be abased, and I know how to abound: every where and in all things I am instructed both to be full and to be hungry, both to abound and to suffer need. 13 I can do all things through Christ which strengtheneth me. You don't have to like your weakness. You don't have to maintain your weakness. You can change with a little help. Don't be mad about having it, do something constructive about it. If you fix it, change it, or get rid of it, you will like the person that you get in return.

Enough about flaws and weaknesses; you need to know your strengths also. Everyone should have something in their life that they are confident about; a central truth about themselves that is a constant. This information is the tangible that gives life balance when the negatives seem to be overwhelming. Knowing your strengths may not win the battle for you, but it can help you avoid losing the battle. However, knowing your strength doesn't help you to love yourself unless you comprehend the limits of that quality. Samson knew of his strength, but he chose to test the limits of it without God and temporarily lost his strength, his sight, and his freedom. Verify what you know, but be willing to relinquish command of situations when you are about to exhaust all of your capabilities. One fault of mankind is they fail to acknowledge when they have exceeded their capabilities then choose not to seek help. Study yourself to understand where you are strong and the countermeasures that can make that strength invalid. For example, if you are strong willed except concerning a specific topic or focus, you have the ammunition to maximize your strength. When you manage your strengths wisely you will feel better about yourself.

Managing your strengths is important because no one but a bully likes a bully. You will feel better about yourself if you control your strength by exposing it and exercising it only when it is absolutely required. This was a trait that Jesus Christ exercised while performing the will of His Father. Having all of the power of heaven and earth at His disposal He could have easily avoided the punishment of the soldiers, the sting of the lashes, and the pain of the cross. But the man/God that walked this earth with the ability to command the wind and the waves held His peace with His strength under control. Yet He exercised it when it was time as He defeated death, hell, and the grave. Had He prematurely exercised His power, we have no idea what the consequences would have been. There are other examples of such extravagance. If a parent severely punishes a child for every offence, then the punishment becomes meaningless. If every issue is the most important in the world and requires full force support, then none of the issues really are important because they all get the same treatment. Managing your strength gives it more emphasis when it is used. That behavior makes you feel better about yourself.

Conceptual Summary

1. Glorifying your weakness to get attention really only gets you a definition of being weak. It has the advantage of gaining you sympathy for a while, but even you won't like the consequences over time.

2. God's favor supersedes any favor you might gain from the masses by belittling yourself. The protocol for false humility is short-lived.

3. Using your weakness as an excuse eventually becomes a lame excuse. Unfortunately, excuses are desirable only to those who provide them. Everyone else wants reasons.

4. Despite the fact that it is not necessary to glorify your weakness, you should know what they are. Knowing them helps you to understand your personal limitations. Knowing your limitations helps you to know when to invoke the awesome power of God.

5. Knowing your limitations and/or weaknesses gives you less reason to feel sorry for yourself if you accept that they are a part of your character.

6. This knowledge should help you avoid venturing into environments where your weaknesses will be exploited. If you know that the smell of alcohol will cause you to desire a drink, stay away from the open bottles.

7. When you have identified the weakness or problem it is necessary to do something about it.

8. Your strength makes balance in a life of weaknesses, but emphasis must be with moderation.

Thought Provoking Queries

1. Are you willing to personally acknowledge your weaknesses?

2. Are you willing to acknowledge your weaknesses without raining pity upon yourself?

3. Once acknowledged, is your weakness something that you are willing to address to the point of repair or resolution?

4. Can you display your strength without bragging about or flaunting it?

5. If you won't address your weakness are you willing to avoid situations where it might be exploited?

Chapter Seven

How Do I Feel About Myself?

To understand yourself and why you perform the way you do, you must ask yourself if you are content with whom you are. Liking the person that you are does not necessarily make you love yourself. Conversely, loving yourself does not indicate that you like yourself, either. You may like the character, emotional make-up and physical capabilities that you have but live in an environment where your make-up is not the acceptable model. This can cause a conflict or paradox. The ugly duckling was completely out of character with the ducks but was perfect with the swans. If your concerns are founded in the opinions of others, you may find that you can never be totally content with whom you are. Such perspective towards yourself can cause you to live double standards just to appease those whom you think are important to you. You allow them to become judge and jury in your life without having an advocate for your defense. The only person worthy of having that much power over your behavior is Jesus Christ. All others should have to accept the product that God made you to be. This information should make you think about whether you are located in the correct environment. Once that is determined, you need to consider whether you require an adjustment or relocation.

Let's imagine the scenario that you have no environmental influences, no one is trying to tell you what to be, and all that governs your opinion of yourself is you. You now require a decision about what you want to be and where you want to go. This decision should be based on your personal convictions. God has given you this power in your past and over your present and future. Your personal characteristics may influence that decision but it is still yours to make. Your purpose in life is the part of you that really determines how much you love the dynamic person you are. Regardless of whether you are blessed with beauty, talent, or intelligence, purpose gives all characteristics of you meaning. It is one reason why serving a divine deity makes a difference in how a person feels about themselves. The emotional highs associated with accomplishment, wealth, fame and recognition are not ingredients to loving one's self; they merely give instantaneous euphoria. This can make you wonder why people who appear to have it all can never get enough and still have issues with themselves. The person who has had fame and finds that it has faded develops issues trying to regain it. Meanwhile, the Christian who finds notoriety but chooses to give God the glory can retire from the spotlight and still be at peace. When the purpose is not to glorify yourself, many of the issues associated with ego, self-esteem, fame, and fortune disappear. Am I implying that you can't really love yourself without God's purpose defined and executed in your life? Well, fulfillment and a sense of accomplishment or completing a purpose bring about a feeling rarely obtained in any other way. The enemy of God's purpose can offer satisfaction but as with the lie in the garden, it can only be temporary at best. To be king of the world for a moment is an exercise in short-termed happiness.

Meanwhile, to learn to love yourself brings long-term peace, contentment, and the sense of fulfillment.

Conceptual Summary

1. Being comfortable in your shell does not necessarily mean that you love yourself. Confidence that you will not be the topic of negative discussion does not indicate self-love.

2. Acceptance and popularity in society are not indicators of love of one's self either. The opinions of others are only important if you happen to know what they are and feel obligated to allow yourself to be evaluated by them.

3. Without external bias, you have the ability to consider how you feel about yourself. It is the most important personal evaluation you can make. The result of that evaluation will determine how you approach everything else in life.

4. Good and important things can occur in your life, but they should not be used to define who you are and how you feel about yourself. The merits of the

present moment are more tangible than the past. Those who meet you today may not know about your history.

5. The characteristics you are blessed with are physical or tangible identifiers but not reasons to love yourself. Should fate remove them from your inventory of blessings, the person inside of you should not change nor should how you feel about that person.

6. The purpose of being does impact how you feel about yourself. If your purpose is merely to bring fame, praise, and glory to yourself, when neither of those conditions are present, the lack of them can cause you to resent or despise yourself.

Thought Provoking Queries

1. Have you identified the positive characteristics about yourself?

2. Are the notable characteristics so profound that you believe them to be reasons to love yourself?

3. Are any of these characteristics associated with your purpose in life?

4. Do you have a purpose for your life, special contribution to society, or your family?

5. Is there fulfillment in the purpose that you have identified for yourself?

Chapter Eight

Why Am I here?

The commitment to purpose has many benefits when they are Godly kingdom based. However, many people have tried to utilize the concept of purpose for selfish ambition. Having purpose will provide you with somewhere to exert your effort, but it may not necessarily give you the benefit that you expect if God is not involved. Creating purpose outside of God can mean that you are creating something else as your god. So as a cautionary warning, be careful about the purposes that you create. Here are some purposes to avoid: someone else's personal happiness, fame and/or fortune from personal notoriety, and to feel superior to someone else. Most of these causes are really beyond your control, and none of them have lasting value to your love of yourself or your personal satisfaction. Only what you do for Christ will last.

So what happens if you have been living the double life – the Clark Kent and Superman lifestyle? You remember what the Bible says about two masters, don't you? **Matthew 6:24 No man can serve two masters: for either he will hate the one, and love the other; or else he will hold to the one, and despise the other. Ye cannot serve God and mammon.** You will find reason to hate or strongly dislike a part of yourself because you cannot be the real you all of the time. This lifestyle is one practiced often in the history of mankind. We really want to be accepted. We really want to blend in with the most acceptable group in our influential society. And when we are associated with two or more spheres of influence we have to work at being accepted in them all. Many times it never occurs to us that our uniqueness is what makes us desirable company anyway. So trying to conform to multiple groups is a waste of our time and to the recipients of our efforts an insult. The Christian approach to this has been simplified by God's word. **Romans 12:1 I beseech**

you therefore, brethren, by the mercies of God, that ye present your bodies a living sacrifice, holy, acceptable unto God, which is your reasonable service. 2 And be not conformed to this world: but be ye transformed by the renewing of your mind, that ye may prove what is that good, and acceptable, and perfect, will of God. Still, when in this kind of situation, we must weigh the consequences of change and decide to proceed at the risk of that commitment. As a Christian you might focus on the rewards instead of the risks. When you decide to be yourself all of the time, there will be consequences. You will have to explain your behavior to all of those groups impacted. Or, you will subject yourself to ridicule and criticism. As you can see the transition could be painful; this is why many people conveniently maintain status quo. If you are reading this and you are a Christian, your mandate is to serve and please one master. All others can find solace in the fact that you may not be what they want or expect but you are consistent. When you choose to be yourself and only yourself, life is simplified and you have more room to love yourself. When you decide to no longer be double-minded the work has just begun. Singleness of purpose requires first that you fully analyze the tools that you have to work with, secondly, what effort that it will take to accomplish the purpose, and, thirdly, the honesty that it takes to be a realist. If your purpose came from God, you must acknowledge that you are the tool, the mechanism, and the vessel that is being used. Despite the fact that you are accustomed to the operation of this bodily shell, only God knows its capabilities and limitations fully.

To investigate purpose and caring for yourself we must understand the sincerity that is required to support your commitment to yourself. There are many things that can only occur when you treat yourself like you need and want to be treated. Waiting for others to show you the love you need will often mean that you get no love at all. Of course someone loves you, but their issues come before yours. They want to see you succeed but not necessarily at their expense. So if you do not show yourself the love, some-times you will be left wanting. Your sincerity towards yourself will help you develop a more concrete feeling of commitment to others. If you allow other things, issues, or another person's purpose to override yours, you lose a portion of your character. That portion of character says that if you cannot honor a commitment to yourself and your purpose, how can you be trusted to honor a commitment to someone else? This was a principle that Jesus Christ emphasized in some of His parables about stewardship. **Matthew 25:21 His lord said unto him, Well done, thou good and faithful servant: thou hast been faithful over a few things, I will make thee ruler over many things: enter thou into the joy of thy lord**. This is really where loving yourself before you attempt to love others starts. You learn how others would like to be treated. Work on loving yourself without becoming selfish and self-centered, and you will be the person that God would have you to be.

Conceptual Summary

1. Making the satisfaction or happiness of another person your purpose in life is beyond your scope of accomplishment and makes no contribution to your love of self. If they happen to blame you for their lack of satisfaction or happiness they have problems with understanding how to love themselves also.

2. When you ask the question of your own purpose for being here you may find that without prior thought there is no defined purpose established. If your self-defined purpose is to be the support mechanism for someone else, then you must ask what happens when they are no longer the prime objective in your life.

3. Living to please someone else, other than your God, is a distraction to any commitment that you may have established for yourself. It seems that when others find out what your purpose is they will always establish that their cause has a higher priority than yours.

4. The effort to serve two masters or to be in bondage to more than one master is an exercise in futility. It is the reason why good parents must develop one mind or directive for their children's guidance.

5. The division between the person you really are and the person that you want others to see can cause more stress than just being disliked for whom you are. Living a double life introduces confusion to the actor.

Thought Provoking Queries

1. Can you separate being a good parent, spouse, or co-worker from child worship, spouse worship and/or career worship?

2. How do you justify the level of commitment and effort to those who assume that they cannot exist without your contributions to their welfare?

3. Assuming that your effort to those causes provides you a sense of satisfaction and purpose, have you considered what will happen to those emotions when those entities no longer require your service? Will you still feel good about yourself?

4. When you are living a double life, how do you know when you are performing because of you?

5. Can you figure out a method to escape that double life and standard?

Chapter Nine

The Replacement Love

We acknowledge, along with you, that someone loves you. At the top of the list, God loves you. You have family, friends and well-wishers that love you, also. But no one will take responsibility for the kind of affection that you need to commit to yourself. That kind of love typically ended when momma potty trained you. From that point on you got good advice, concerned guidance, and sometimes loving suggestions that you had to follow through with, for your own good. For example, the doctor may tell you that you need to eat at least one apple per day; this expresses his or her concern for your well-being. However, that doctor cannot take a single bite for you because the execution portion is your responsibility. Good intentions do not indicate real love. A friend

could be with you at the doctors' office, hear his sugges-
tion, buy you the apples, and remind you that you need
to eat one. But if you refuse to consume the apple, the
love falls short. This is one of the things that happen with
New Year's resolutions. We have good intentions but the
love for ourselves apparently is overruled by something
of greater importance and significance. We don't normally
observe from that perspective because we like to chalk
it up to changing our minds. However, telling ourselves
that we changed our minds is really lying to ourselves.
And of course lying to yourself doesn't really hurt anyone,
does it? Actually it does; it hurts you. The lie exposes that
you have broken a promise to yourself. The lie blatantly
displays that you did not accomplish what you declared
that you would accomplish for yourself. You have to compensate for the loss in some way. If you set this pattern
with yourself, it will be easy to impose this behavior on
others. Furthermore, lying to yourself defeats the love
requirement by shoveling deceit into the equation. The
lie becomes self-betrayal instead of self-love. It also puts
you lower on the love chain, making you both the bully

and victim and gives you little opportunity to recoup. This becomes a vicious cycle.

So, fulfilling a commitment to yourself is an expression of loving yourself. It will help you to confirm that in your mind no one else is better than you. Now you are just as important as the next person. Completing a defined purpose for yourself is an expression of love for yourself. It gives that sense of accomplishment that boosts the ego and brings about self-assurance. Being honest with yourself is an expression of love for yourself. Telling yourself the truth is the beginning of dispelling lies. By starting with yourself, the truth is now exposed and makes it easier to expose it to others. **John 8:31 Then said Jesus to those Jews which believed on him, If ye continue in my word, then are ye my disciples indeed; 32 And ye shall know the truth, and the truth shall make you free.** This scripture makes the assumption that you are a believer, and that you have a need for the truth. You require the truth to make informed decisions about yourself. The truth gives you a baseline to proceed from and solid information for analysis. But it also exposes the portions of your character that need to be addressed to make you feel better about yourself.

Next you must take responsibility for your actions. You must determine whether your actions were acceptable to you or not. Try to make that determination without imposing shame, guilt, or punishment on yourself. Accept that what you did was done by you and is merely a fact. **Galatians 6:7 Be not deceived; God is not mocked: for whatsoever a man soweth, that shall he also reap. 8 For he that soweth to his flesh shall of the flesh reap corruption; but he that soweth to the Spirit shall of the Spirit reap life everlasting. 9 And let us not be weary in well doing: for in due season we shall reap, if we faint not. 10 As we have therefore opportunity, let us do good unto all men, especially unto them who are of the household of faith.** The consequences of your actions will be consistent with the activity. The consequences are coming if we continue to pursue that objective. You define the purpose and you execute it, whether successfully or with opportunity for improvement. Now the consequences must be acknowledged, accepted, and part of life.

Second guessing because the results were not satisfying enough and wishing you had done something else does not change what you did. Attempting to shift the blame or responsibility to someone else does not change what you did. Taking credit for or acknowledging your actions and behavior is the first step toward feeling better about yourself; not necessarily the actions that you took.

What happens when you are trying your best, and you don't like the results? Most of the time, we beat ourselves up and speculate on what could have happened if we had done something differently. Unfortunately, you have no control over the past; you can only review it to analyze your mistakes and try desperately to never commit them again. Reviewing your mistakes won't make you feel better about yourself, but the process can help you move forward. The biggest problem you face is acknowledging to yourself that you made the mistake and not attempting to shift the blame, assign shame, or carry the embarrassment associated with the mistake. All of these only add to your dislike for yourself. The example you need to follow is King David after he had sinned. He mourned the loss of his son for a time period and then moved on with his future. Do not hold a grudge against yourself. Forgive yourself and let it go. Remember that forgiving yourself sets the pattern for forgiving others. **Mark 11:25 And when ye stand praying, forgive, if ye have ought against any: that your Father also which is in heaven may forgive you your trespasses. 26 But if ye do not forgive, neither will your Father which is in heaven forgive your trespasses.** If you can't forgive yourself, what priority do others have for getting your pardon? Since no one but God can be more important to you than yourself, what place would the neighbors and the rest of the world have? As you look at what you have done to yourself, you can see the predicament that God has with you. He sees your sin or mistake and as soon as you ask for forgiveness He instantly separates that issue as far from you as the east is from the west; a distance that we really can't comprehend. So you have to learn to forgive yourself in order to love yourself.

Don't let your mistakes instill fear into your being. Just because you failed once doesn't indict you to being an eternal failure. The perspective should be that no matter where you come from, the path before you is a fresh trail. The path before you does not contain the debris of the trail behind although it may contain different obstacles. As a Christian you have God in you and He is not associated with failure. Let the God in you navigate and lead you into the truths that you require to be successful. It may seem difficult to forget the things of the past because they have left their mark on your life. Although the mark may remain, there are objectives ahead that require your attention just like the Apostle Paul in his letter to the church at Philippi. **Philippians 3:13 Brethren, I count not myself to have apprehended: but this one thing I do, forgetting those things which are behind, and reaching forth unto those things which are before, 14 I press toward the mark for the prize of the high calling of God in Christ Jesus.** You need to shift your focus from the mark made to the mark you are to make. For example, the pitcher who has just walked the batter before now has to concentrate on striking out the batter in front of him. Imagine the doubt that would be apparent if he thought about how he had pitched four balls to the last batter rather than focusing on pitching strikes to the new batter. He would be operating in fear that he might walk another batter. On the contrary, the cook who messed up a recipe last time would remember that he messed up, only to try to analyze what he did wrong and desperately try not to make the same mistake again. Let the mistake be a lesson but not a threat. Learn from your past mistakes; move on to victory and a greater love for yourself.

Conceptual Summary

1. Unfortunately, you must take responsibility for supplying affection to yourself. You have the option of allowing an external person to supply a portion of that affection to you but ultimately, you determine how much and what kind of love you need and then when you need that love.

2. Honesty to yourself is a key ingredient to loving yourself, improving your self-esteem, and possessing the ability to modify either emotion. You can choose to live a lie, but should you ever remove the layers of untruth the person who remains is you.

3. Lying to yourself sets a dangerous trend that can impact your interaction with others. This interaction will lead to substituting reality for the instant gratification of false compliments to make you feel better about yourself.

4. Fulfilling your commitment to yourself is an act of displaying your love of yourself to yourself. Any distraction from that objective is self-defeating and the beginning of other symptoms that indicate self-hate.

5. Despite any importance, clout or priority that you may acknowledge in other human beings you should acknowledge the same for yourself. Their characteristics and qualities may be commendable, but they don't live inside you. You don't even have to mimic their traits to feel good about who you are.

6. The level of affection needed to sustain wholesomeness is different in everyone. Because you are the only one who can define that requirement, only you can determine how much is needed from inside and where you will receive the remainder of it.

7. Taking responsibility for your actions is an honorable quality that can give you joy and/or pain. However, it is a practice that will help you know who you are, address issues that require attention, and alleviate concerns about blame.

8. There are incidents and events that you are responsible for that will require you to be willing to forgive yourself. If you choose to maintain the guilt, you will be plagued with it for life.

Thought Provoking Queries

1. Do you know how you feel about yourself?

2. Have you considered all of the sources of affection that impact your life? Has it always been enough?

3. After you filter out all of the opinions of others, are you honest with yourself about the amount of affection that you need?

4. Have you determined what percentage of your required affection comes from you?

5. Do you consider commitments to yourself as important as your commitments to others?

6. Do you lie to yourself about any personal issues?

7. Are you ready to accept responsibility for the failures, mistakes and bad decisions that you have made? Will that acceptance impact your ability to forgive yourself?

Chapter Ten

The Internal Search When Things Are Awry

Next, associated with mistakes and the barrage of continued unfortunate circumstances and situations the 'woe is me' syndrome or self-pity is developed. It is perfectly okay to acknowledge for analysis purposes that things have gone awry for you. The assessment will give you information to support your life improvement plans. However, to dwell on such things brings on this self-pity and can cause one to dislike or not love themselves, especially when they blame themselves for the events that have occurred. This perspective is akin to worry and unjustified concern. Blaming yourself for your plight should only be considered when you are the initiator or motivator of the circumstances or events. Sometimes you are in the circumstances and situations through no fault of your own. Instead of dwelling on the fact that you are there, convert that energy into thinking of or seeking ways to get out of it. Energy wasted on self-pity could be used to consider solutions to your plight.

Self-pity leads to depression and stress. The impact on your physical being can be extremely undesirable; unexplained illness, negative attitudes and poor disposition are all symptoms. All three are conditions that indicate that you are not necessarily in a position to love yourself. Many use self-pity to solicit reaction or response from those around them. And as the self-pity escalates, the expectation of attention grows. Self-pity can get you attention, but normally it is not the long-term gratification that you may truly be seeking, because after a while that attention turns to resentment. When attention turns to resentment, the sources of your attention will find reasons not to be around you at all, causing you to feel even more pity. So the next time that you start feeling like Charlie Brown (it's raining on me and no one else) brush the clouds away by seeking the Lord for joy. **Hebrews 13:5 Let your conversation be**

without covetousness; and be content with such things as ye have: for he hath said, I will never leave thee, nor forsake thee. 6 So that we may boldly say, The Lord is my helper, and I will not fear what man shall do unto me. The Lord is there to help you even with your insecurities and self-pity.

Remember that self-pity is a choice. Most of the time when you choose not to focus on solutions and escape from the circumstance, you dwell on the causes of the problem, who to blame, and the 'what if's' of the circumstance. As you think about them more, they grow in magnitude and so does your dislike for yourself. Make a choice to study the resolution which is hard enough work by itself. However, sometimes you cannot see the path out of your circumstance because the hedges of the environment hide the escape. It is during these types of circumstances that you must learn dependence on God Almighty. He has the weed-eater that cuts the path for your freedom. Getting out will make you feel better about yourself, but learning to lean on God will give you greater confidence for you future helping you to love yourself even more.

Before we proceed, it is necessary to present a definition to justify certain types of behavior. Consider the difference between self-preservation and selfishness. Self-preservation is the act of naturally doing what is necessary to survive. It is not something that you have the opportunity to think about; it occurs involuntarily as a protection for your being. One example of self-preservation is you are thrown into a mass of water, your body will fight to stay alive whether you can swim or not. There is nothing selfish about self-preservation; it is normal. It is evident that selfishness is not an act of self-preservation. It is more an act of fear and greed. It fosters several other undesirable characteristics in mankind. We will discuss them in detail so that you will be able to recognize these traits in yourself and in others. It will help you to understand loving yourself even more.

Conceptual Summary

1. Bad things happen to everyone. Despite the fact that they may have happened to you, bad issues and events do not warrant bad feelings or self-pity. The

consequence of feeling bad about your situation or circumstance and developing self-pity only leads to other unwanted by-products and self-hate.

2. Blame is not necessary in order to find solutions nor is it a required element to acquire closure. Taking responsibility for your actions does not necessarily lead to the reason for a circumstance or situation. Removing blame from the equation may relieve your associated discomfort.

3. Broadcasted self-pity only gains a display of sympathy prior to unwarranted resentment. To seek sympathy can add embarrassment to the list of shortcomings that others see in you.

4. It is your choice to feel sorry for yourself. You have the power within to dictate how you feel about yourself without considering any outside influences, whether tangible, implied, or imposed.

Thought Provoking Queries

1. Do you harbor self-pity? Are the reasons justified from your perspective?

2. Have you considered the by-products of the self-pity that you consider reasonable in your life?

3. Do you broadcast your self-pity to gain sympathy or attention from your friends, family and associates? How long can you put up the act?

4. Have you made a choice to pity yourself? Why?

Chapter Eleven

The Unselfish Divide

What if your personal circumstances and situation appear to be fine, but you cannot figure out why you still don't really love yourself very well? Despite having it all, knowing it all, and managing it all, sometimes the problem develops from wanting to keep it all. That effort to keep it all or to keep others from getting any portion of it is the foundation of selfishness. **Ezekiel 34:18 *Seemeth it* a small thing unto you to have eaten up the good pasture, but ye must tread down with your feet the residue of your pastures? and to have drunk of the deep waters, but ye must foul the residue with your feet? 19 And *as for* my flock, they eat that which ye have trodden with your feet; and they drink that which ye have fouled with your feet. 20 Therefore thus saith**

the Lord GOD unto them; Behold, I, *even* **I, will judge between the fat cattle and between the lean cattle. 21 Because ye have thrust with side and with shoulder, and pushed all the diseased with your horns, till ye have scattered them abroad; 22Therefore will I save my flock, and they shall no more be a prey; and I will judge between cattle and cattle.** Selfishness carries with it several other character traits and issues that can cause a person not to be happy with themselves and thus not love themselves. First of all, selfishness exploits the principle that God provides more than enough resource with reason. One important reason to avoid selfishness is that everything on earth is perishable. You cannot take any of it with you when you die. Also, those who are blessed with abundance are expected to bless others with some of their substance. Determining if, when, and why to bless others, can be the major contributor to the attitude of selfishness. That concept was included in the Mosaic Law.

The first deterrent to unselfishness is the feeling of being used or exploited. No matter how kind hearted you may be or how willing you are to give or share, you can feel abused in the process. If you feel like you are being taken advantage of, you will lean towards being selfish and denying your service and gifts to others. The conflict of wanting to help but not wanting to feel used can contribute to you not feeling very good about yourself. This situation actually creates stress in your life. To overcome and avoid this issue, certain steps must be taken to alleviate the cause for the stress. If you really don't mind being a benefactor to someone else but they seem to delight in exploiting your goodwill, develop an understanding through communication with the persons involved. **Proverbs 4:7 Wisdom is the principle thing; therefore get wisdom: and with all thy getting get understanding. 8 Exalt her, and she shall promote thee: she shall bring thee to honour, when thou dost embrace her. 9 She shall give to thine head an ornament of grace: a crown of glory shall she deliver to thee.** Since you are the giver, it is your privilege to explain to the recipient of your contributions the rules of engagement. If they reject the rules, then you are justified in being "selfish". Setting those ground rules will give you more peace of mind and will deter hard feelings when you refuse to provide the request or solicited gift.

Being taken advantage of is a feeling that generates an atmosphere of self-hate. You can hate yourself for letting yourself be explioted. You can develop a grudge against the one taking advantage of you. And this feeling or environment will follow you so that each time you are in the presence of those who have taken advantage of you, you feel intimidated. You do not love yourself when you allow your hurts to be hidden and to grow.

You might wonder how you got to be selfish. There is no special trait that indicates that you will be selfish; it seems to be a characteristic that is developed due to life changing events that occur in your life. No one knows what will have a lasting impact on your character, except God. As speculation, it could have come from remembering your past where the portions that were available were never enough or you were forced to share against your will. **Ecclesiastes 1:8 All things are full of labour; man cannot utter it: the eye is not satisfied with seeing, nor the ear filled with hearing. 9 The thing that hath been, it is that which shall be; and that which is done is that which shall be done: and there is no new thing**

Love Yourself

under the sun. 10 Is there any thing whereof it may be said, See, this is new? it hath been already of old time, which was before us. 11 There is no remembrance of former things; neither shall there be any remembrance of things that are to come with those that shall come after. If you came from a situation where there was never enough, you can begin to believe that there will never be enough. If you came from an environment where you were forced to share against your will, you may continue to believe that you will be forced to share against your will. You didn't just happen upon this feeling of selfishness; it was planted in your life and requires uprooting. For the individual that never had enough, it is only a natural feeling that they need to hoard in order to compensate for that condition. The hoarder never considers that they can only use so much; their thought pattern revolves around satisfying their inner mind-set that requires that they get more, since they never know when the need will surface and they are without something. This can really happen to those who have been lacking for a large part of their life. When the opportunity comes that allows them to acquire wealth they really want to over-compensate for the times when they had nothing. They will pursue extensive careers in order to fulfill that ambition without regard for family, friends or colleagues. They tend to forget that they need people to survive. It is only when they take a breather, do they realize that they have no one worthy with whom to share their experiences and wealth. The loneliness contributes to their emptiness and lack of love for themselves. Ironically, during their quest to get more and more they really thought that they loved themselves.

Selfishness is often not understood in marriage relationships. The concept goes beyond the obvious because it impacts the lives of many and is perceived to be normal. To better understand marriage and selfishness one must review the plan of God for those who are married. When that plan is executed, the quality of life is enhanced, the family structure is strengthened, and faith in God is solidified. When a couple chooses to pursue wealth to achieve personal gain or lofty goals by both partners working, it all appears to be normal. However, this idea is the foundation for selfishness and a defiance of the plan of God for their lives. Quality of life suffers when partners ignore or defy their God-given roles in the relationship. The self-ishness does not expose itself until later in life when the levels of neglect are defined by those who were left alone. Many people don't think about the love and care that they should have given to their family and to their relationship until they are wishing that they could receive some sort of support in old age. Don't beat yourself up wishing you had spent more time with family because it is a waste of time. Despite your efforts to possess the luxuries of life to maintain social status and comfort, someone will recognize that they would have enjoyed your company more than the stuff. While you have the opportunity, think about the price you pay for the alleged wealth that you sacrificed to achieve. This effort at loving yourself is definitely a long-term projection.

Those who were forced to share despite their wish not to at the time, feel like it's their right and privilege to be selfish now. Without an authority figure over them to force the issue, they can now withhold whatever they choose. Living out this behavior makes them feel like they have reestablished their identity, although in reality there is hurt under the surface of their being. This effort at rebellion seems like a righteous behavior because it appears to be harmless to others. It is displayed in several ways. Rather than share a portion of what they have, a selfish person is more willing to purchase a new one for someone else. Or instead of tempting the other person with a desire, the selfish person hides the object to avoid being asked to share; obviously others won't ask for something they don't know exists. Unfortunately, the selfish seed develops a plant that is corrupted with the characteristic of the seed. What starts out as something simple and innocent can grow into a lifetime behavior. And although someone in your past may have tried to rid you of the stronghold, they only cultivated it making you worse. The obvious cure for your stronghold is to ask God for deliverance and the power to forgive those who attempted to force you to share and to forgive yourself. If you really have enough to share, you are blessed, and it is the will of God that you do so.

There are times when the request to share is out of your own need and other times the request to share is from your abundance. When you are asked to share out of your own need, you can justifiably resist in the name of self-preservation. Our best example of such is in **Matthew 25:8 And the foolish said unto the wise, Give us of your oil; for our lamps are gone out. 9 But the wise answered, saying, Not so; lest there be not enough for us and you: but go ye rather to them that sell, and buy for yourselves. 10 And while they went to buy, the bridegroom came; and they that were ready went in with him to the marriage: and the door was shut.** So it is not selfish to pay your own bills before you consider helping someone else. Nor, is it selfish to make sure that you have enough to eat before you invite others to your dinner table. However, if you can assess the situation and conclude that their need is greater than yours, sharing may be the consideration before you decide to maintain for self-preservation reasons. This really comes down to a choice of character; the willingness to sacrifice a portion of your need to appease the need of someone else. You probably would welcome such sacrifice if you were the needy one. However, sharing out of your need only displays love for yourself if you are one that desires to be praised with gratitude for your efforts. When that gratitude doesn't come, you will feel used instead. This is a concept to consider when attempting loving your neighbor.

The selfish have a slightly different perspective on receiving their abundance. It starts with the attitude that because I worked for this; you'll have to work to get your own. The justification for this attitude and perspective is the fear that there might be a need in the future that won't be fulfilled because you had it and you gave it away. Some might say they're saving for a rainy day and have no idea how much is enough. Another example is having only enough for me because I like everything that I have. Or, you haven't shared yours so why should I share mine with you? These are childish perspectives that typically generate resentment. Selfishness can alienate you from those who might be there for you in a time of need. The projected persona gives those around you the perception that you are selfish, and they should stay away from you and your stuff. This contributes to your loneliness and ultimately a feeling of despair. You have stuff, but your circle of support is rapidly shrinking.

Sharing out of your abundance should be easier than out of your needs. However, this concept takes on different responsibilities because usually the sharer has the privilege of discriminating between whom he or she may share. This individual may use selfishness in a different manner. They may share with the idea of gaining favor from that opportunity. And when they acknowledge that they will gain nothing, they will give nothing. This seems to be in their rights and authority to control. It gives a feeling of superiority to that person to laud over others while fostering their selfish ambition. You would not want to be a victim of such treatment unless you were fortunate enough to be receiving what you desired from them. Be careful with this type of selfishness because when you are found out your circle of influence will diminish causing you to question your love for yourself.

Conceptual Summary

1. Acquisition of personal possessions does not guarantee that you will love yourself or be happy. Furthermore, the quest to keep your personal pos-

sessions or trophies to yourself will only be preoc-cupation that will leave you with less time to address your personal affection requirements.

2. Fear of exploitation can make you appear to be selfish and contribute to undue stresses. Being a benefactor can generate these fears especially when you observe that you are being abused because of your charitable heart.

3. As the benefactor, you have the right to establish the rules of engagement associated with your tan-gible gifts and services. These rules, if enforced, will assist you in avoiding feelings of abuse and exploitation.

4. Personal trophies and higher social status do not equate to a higher quality of life. Substituting finance and what it can provide in exchange for a wholesome and full home lifestyle, usually back-fires when that type of lifestyle is most needed. It emphasizes instantaneous satisfaction of desires instead of contentment with having what is needed which is a very selfish perspective.

5. Self-preservation is a right and the expectation while selfishness is merely a practiced desire.

Thought Provoking Queries

1. Are you considered to be selfish by others in your circle of influence? Do you accept this labeling?

2. Have you considered why you are identified as being selfish? Have you been this way for a long period of time?

3. Have you determined within yourself the amount of personal possessions that constitute having enough?

4. Is the abundance something that you could share without personal grief or discomfort?

5. Have you considered that within your inventory of possessions there are items that you haven't used, needed, or missed for over a year?

Chapter Twelve

It's a Personal Thing

Now is the time to proceed from studying how you cooperate with others to how you treat yourself. For many of us the only consideration we give ourselves is the care we take so that others won't be offended by our presence. We are diligent in the care we give ourselves in order that we are accepted and not rejected by making sure that our appearance is up to expected standards, that we are reasonably punctual within the limits of our associates, and that we are fashionably attired with the right brands, etc. Sometimes Christians go overboard with this in trying to be accepted by both the secular society and the Christian world, but it is a part of life that can cause us a measure of contentment. Still, making others accept you won't necessarily make you love yourself. So, in order to enhance your feelings about yourself, there needs to be some time and ideals set aside just for you. Occasionally, you will need to think about your situation to completely understand your position so you can effectively determine where you wish to go. Outside input can assist in this but only you can give a fair assessment. They are on the outside looking in while you are on the inside looking out. They can only see as much as you allow of the inside activity. You may share this time with others but even if they aren't around, you still need this outlet for yourself. Within these parameters you require time to rest. Sleep is a part of self-preservation; rest is more focused on winding down or catching your breathe. Although you may think that the world will stop turning if you don't get the task achieved, you will stop moving if you don't reserve some time for rest. With the exception of immediate life and death situations, everything will wait until you have the time to get to it. Life is not always in crisis mode. Everything is not the most important thing of the moment, and the urgency label can be reserved for the time when you have prioritized the list of things to do. Working so hard that you simply fall asleep wherever you sit down should only happen occasionally. This is not to condone laziness; just make sure that you don't overdo the working part either.

Everyone should have a hobby to release stress. Typically the people of the secular world tend to go overboard here in order to avoid being bored. Christians don't have the luxury of entertaining an abundance of hobbies because they should have set aside some quiet time to be with God, some devotion to kingdom building or ministry, and some quality time with family or love ones. However, reading a book, getting some exercise, or maybe developing a talent is fine example of inexpensive hobbies. If your only outlet is watching television, you need to find something else to release your stress. Watching television is more related to getting rest than a constructive hobby. However a good hobby will give you a sense of fulfillment and make you feel better about yourself.

Be careful about what you use for fulfillment and about where you seek or find it. To help you with this assignment, you must understand the purpose of the event, commitment, or activity where you are seeking fulfillment in. **Proverbs 3:13 Happy is the man that findeth wisdom, and the man that getteth understanding. 14 For the merchandise of it is better than the merchandise of silver, and the gain thereof than fine gold. 15 She is more precious than rubies: and all the things thou canst desire are not to be compared unto her.** If you are seeking fulfillment at your place of employment, you are there for the wrong purpose. It is nice that you like your job and even nicer that you like the people that you work with, but that is not why you are there. You are not at work to find your sense of purpose in typing or turning a wrench. You are there to gain the financial resources to keep you alive and to maintain your current quality of life after you leave your place of employment. If the job pays you properly and enough, that is all the fulfillment of that entity that you require. Feel blessed that the people who work with you think that you are great. Feel blessed that your boss thinks that you are doing a good job for him as you are supposed to do. But don't allow the job to be your source of fulfillment because you could lose it. Over committing to work to gain trinkets can make you think that the job is paramount to life. However, the reality is that if you are so committed to working that you are always at work, you don't have time to enjoy any of what you earned. If your world revolves around your place of employment, what recourse do you have when that place of employment decides to dissolve? These concepts should make you realize that you have more to relate to than a job.

Try not to find your fulfillment in another person or to live your life through another person. The unfortunate truth is people will let you down and if you use them to find your own self-fulfillment you may wind up despising them and hating yourself. Some people find their fulfillment in the association with a team or sport; the results can be both temporarily rewarding and disappointing. But this is one example that should strongly indicate that people have no guaranteed built-in success factor. It may not appear to be possible, but history shows that it is not unusual for parents to try to live their personal dream through the lives of their children. The child is highly susceptible to parental influence early in life so it can appear that they want what the parent wants. Subsequently, the parent can supply the props, be the support mechanism, and even provide coaching to get the child to achieve the dream that the parent had for themselves but could not realize. For the child, this condition may not remain a viable way of thinking, but the parent of that child can begin to believe that the child really wants the same thing as they do. The problem with living for someone else and their dream is that one day you could and should develop dreams of your own. Furthermore, any setback by the puppet will hurt you the puppetmaster more than it actually hurts the puppet. Pray for the best in others but do not seek your fulfillment in their life or performance.

As to finding your fulfillment in another person, the Bible has a strict rule against such behavior for Christians. **Exodus 20:3 Thou shalt have no other gods before me. 4 Thou shalt not make unto thee any graven image, or any likeness of any thing that is in heaven above, or that is in the earth beneath, or that is in the water under the earth: 5 Thou shalt not bow down thyself to them, nor serve them: for I the LORD thy God am a jealous God, visiting the iniquity of the fathers upon the children unto the third and fourth generation of them**

that hate me; 6 And showing mercy unto thousands of them that love me, and keep my commandments. Only the Almighty God has the right to govern your behavior to such levels. Some of the romantic statements made about special people and relationships indicate that we can indeed reverence individuals so highly that they are treated and respected as gods. And initially we get pleasure out of serving them and lavishing gifts and affection on them. The by-product of such behavior seems to be resentment by that person towards you and eventual abuse and misuse of their position. You may be blinded by your affection for this individual, but when you finally acknowledge that you are being mistreated, you will resent your own actions for the time that you spent allegedly loving them. You will gain this knowledge when your other friends describe to you how abused you really are. Or, the knowledge can be obtained when your object of affection decides that they no longer want what you offer them. In either case you will feel abandoned and unloved by them and less love for yourself.

Conceptual Summary

1. We do many things in this life in order to gain the acceptance of our fellow man or woman. This practice is suitable for protocol, but it should not be a determining factor in how you feel about yourself. The image that you present to gain acceptance from society, can be influenced by too many factors to become the standard for self-acceptance.

2. What others may think of you will change with the seasons or fads. If you choose to allow their opinions to dictate how you feel about yourself, you will be subject to an ever changing perspective of yourself and unpredictable doubts.

3. Personal time is paramount to maintaining healthy feelings, assessments, and stress relief for yourself. Occasionally, you will need to think about your situation to completely understand your position so you can effectively determine where you wish to go. Outside input can assist in this but only you can give a fair assessment. They are on the outside looking

in while you are on the inside looking out. They can only see as much as you allow of the inside activity.

4. For most, personal time should include a hobby for stress relief.

5. For the Christian, the image that you display should not be a cause for your neighbor to falter or stumble, but your first responsibility is to ensure that you remain standing.

6. Having purpose or a reason to obtain fulfillment is a necessary part of well-being. Where or how you seek fulfillment is important to that objective. Finding your purpose in the wrong idea can lead to other problems.

7. You are often challenged to be the main benefactor to an individual; carefully avoid idolizing that person or persons. A human god is difficult to please.

Thought Provoking Queries

1. What value do you place on the opinions of your peers, friends, and family?

2. Have you considered that your peers, friends, and family may have an agenda attached to their broad-casted opinion of you and your value?

3. How do you feel about the purpose from which you derive fulfillment? Is that purpose effectively fulfilling the assigned objective?

4. Have you set aside and defined personal time to address your needs, stress relief, and relaxation requirement?

5. Have you idolized someone for whom you were the benefactor? Is their status so lofty that you are more slave than servant to them?

6. What position in the hierarchy of people, things, and events have you placed yourself?

7. Although there may be concepts with a priority greater than you, do you find yourself challenged

to make yourself last in everything in all your involvements?

Chapter Thirteen

I Am Not the Sum of My Trophies

C areers and significant others provide a world of other possibilities. The existence of things that are substitutes for God is ever present and their usage in His place is an exercise in futility. There are manmade objects that some people choose to seek fulfillment in, to the point of relying on them for good fortune. The reliability of stuff is questionable when you consider that most stuff is created by imperfect creatures and with an expiration date attached. Other objects of superstition are even less reliable for the purpose of finding fulfillment. The lucky rabbit's foot finds that the rabbit wasn't lucky, etc. If God doesn't give it to you, the stuff always has a built-in failure rate. For decades Toyota was considered to be one of the most reliable vehicles on the road, and then came the biggest recall in the history of automobiles. American banks were supposed to be solid as rock until the recent economic meltdown that caused a need for massive bailout by the government. **Psalms 20:5 We will rejoice in thy salvation, and in the name of our God we will set up our banners: the LORD fulfil all thy petitions. 6 Now know I that the LORD saveth his anointed; he will hear him from his holy heaven with the saving strength of his right hand. 7 Some trust in chariots, and some in horses: but we will remember the name of the LORD our God. 8 They are brought down and fallen: but we are risen, and stand upright.** People and stuff will let you down. And even if you gained a sense of fulfillment from some activity, involvement, or commitment, that fulfillment will still leave you with a question of what's next. This implies that the fulfillment that you get from things outside the kingdom of God is always temporary. It equates to the fifteen minutes of fame that everyone speak of. Enjoy it while it lasts but know that you will want something more. You need a sense of purpose and achievement to help you feel complete.

Some find fulfillment or satisfaction in receiving. Most of the time, it feels good to receive, unless you are the extremely proud. The extremely proud only feel a sense of humility or the guilt of owing a return gift or favor. The rest are waiting and hoping to receive something as often as possible. These people are so focused on receiving that they become dependent upon the sources of the benevolence to the point of believing that it is their right and expectation to constantly be on the receiving end of every transaction. Their mindset is that they constantly deserve or they are thinking about what is in the act for them. It is a wonderful life as long as things are going as expected, but any challenge towards fulfillment of that attitude becomes a personal matter. When they don't receive what they think they deserve, the blame game begins, and it is never really the recipient's fault that they didn't receive. You would wonder how this affects their love for themselves. It makes them analyze others opinions of them. The giver didn't give because he or she has a problem with me. The giver didn't give because he or she didn't really understand how important their gift was to me. How can I change their opinion of me so that I can be back on their list of recipients? This person is a user and a taker and usually has no regard for anyone other than themselves. But it hurts when you don't find fulfillment, whether at someone else's expense or your own. Failure breeds contempt and self-hate. Unfortunately, both the user and taker have to be given a rude awakening in order to change. Their expectations are never impacted until they start losing the sources of their benefits. The typical user or taker has developed a conglomerate of stories that push the buttons of their benefactors to the point of persuasion. When the benefactors start to disappear the users and takers stories become more compelling. If that doesn't meet the need, they search for new benefactors. When that no longer works they become depressed and disillusioned because the benefactor was their friend as long as they could count on them to provide. When the well runs dry, they can blame themselves for loosing that source. Long before they reach this stage of life the user and taker needs a real encounter with God. His promise is that He will never leave nor forsake you. As you focus on Him, you will find that you love yourself even more.

The user or taker does not deal with criticism very well. Any effort to show them that they are hurting others usually indicates to them that you are no longer on their list of benefactors and that you are meddling in their business. How well you deal with criticism can severely impact your love for yourself whether you are a taker or not. Unless you are a spoiled brat, you have had to deal with some form of criticism all of your life. You can label it as you wish, but someone or something has pointed out to you that your way is not necessarily the correct way. As Christians, we deal with criticism every time that we open our Bibles; only the perfect man is exempt. If you take every criticism personally, because you happen to be a perfectionist, you may find that life is most difficult. But despite the standards of God, society, and life, it is the criticisms or corrections that make us better. Unfortunately, someone has to have the job of pointing out the flaws, faults, and mistakes that we make. We are responsible for accepting, filtering through analysis, and acting on that criticism. It is the source of the criticism that actually cares about your well-being. King David understood criticism and equated it to severe correction. **Psalms 94:11 The LORD**

knoweth the thoughts of man, that they are vanity. 12 Blessed is the man whom thou chastenest, O LORD, and teachest him out of thy law; 13 That thou mayest give him rest from the days of adversity, The criticism is there to help you, if you use it. If you choose not to use it, the consequences are your responsibility. If your decision causes calamity in your life, you subject yourself to the possibility of receiving the gloating phrase 'I told you so'. But that is not part of the criticism. Because many of us despise being wrong, incorrect, or misunderstood, we can take criticism as a personal and direct attack on our character and our performance. Then we apply self-pity and second guessing or blame ourselves.

Conceptual Summary

1. Having things, no matter how glorious they may be, will not make you have affection for yourself. Trophies may give the sense of accomplishment but the love may still be missing.

2. Assigning value to the possessions will not guarantee that you will have affection for yourself, a

permanent sense of accomplishment, or lasting fulfillment. Temporary euphoria is all that is gained; tomorrow a new requirement will surface.

3. It is not wrong to be on the receiving end of the benevolence process, therefore there is no reason to feel bad. There are several reasons to receive: God could have directed the benevolence, it could just be your turn, your need has to be addressed, or you actually asked for what you received.

4. It is not wise to allow yourself to become totally dependent upon someone, other than God Almighty, being your continuous benefactor. Even if it is their assigned role in your life, it feels good to occasionally have an independent moment. If gives your benefactor a brief reprieve and temporarily removes the feeling that you are enslaved.

5. The urgency of your need often dictates the passion of your request, but the passion exerted can lead to shame if you are not careful. You have the expectancy to present your petition without degrading yourself.

6. Being able to deal with constructive criticism is often necessary for you to develop into the person that you would like to love. Ignoring constructive criticism usually means that you will encounter it again.

Thought Provoking Queries

1. Are you allowing the trophies that you have obtained to dominate how you feel about yourself? If so, what will you do when the trophies are no longer available?

2. Have you learned to accept benevolence gracefully?

3. Can you handle the fact that some benefactors will keep their benevolence to you ever present?

4. Do you feel that you require assistance with every aspect of your life? Are you respectful of the person or persons who supply that support?

5. Can you accept constructive criticism without developing a chip on your shoulder or lasting hurt feelings?

Chapter Fourteen

The Self Critic

S ome situations require that we acknowledge our fault so that we can immediately address the issue. However, acknowledgement and blame are two different perspectives about an issue. For Christians, we acknowledge our faults and repent. We are not concerned with blame or cause because the guilt was nailed to the cross with Christ. Typically we associate blame with psychology and the process of returning to the beginning of an event or thing so that we can eventually find closure through understanding the whole story. Whether you blame Adam or Eve, sin is in our nature so there is no need for discovering the source of our predicament. But our personal dealings with criticism, acknowledgement, and blame can determine how you feel about correction and yourself. The best thing to do with criticism is to analyze it and act appropriately. **II Kings 5:10 And Elisha sent a messenger unto him, saying, Go and wash in Jordan seven times, and thy flesh shall come again to thee, and thou shalt be clean. 11 But Naaman was wroth, and went away, and said, Behold, I thought, He will surely come out to me, and stand, and call on the name of the LORD his God, and strike his hand over the place, and recover the leper. 12 Are not Abana and Pharpar, rivers of Damascus, better than all the waters of Israel? may I not wash in them, and be clean? So he turned and went away in a rage. 13 And his servants came near, and spake unto him, and said, My father, if the prophet had bid thee do some great thing, wouldest thou not have done it? how much rather then, when he saith to thee, Wash, and be clean?** What an example of direct criticism! Naaman was forced to analyze the information for his own good; criticism is like that. Sometimes the proper action is to do nothing because the criticism given does not warrant any activity. Other times compromise is required and therefore more analysis is the order. Then sometimes immediate action is the only recourse. None of these actions or behavior requires that you assign personal blame to the criticism. None of these require that you beat yourself up because you were wrong. None of these require that you revisit the issue over and over to worry about the associated decisions that you made because of the criticism. The commitment to worry and to blame will make you love yourself even less.

Dealing with criticism can also mean that you must understand and deal with your toughest critic – you. Within this concept lies hidden the desire to be loved. When you feel that you are not loved, it becomes easy not to love yourself. This fits within the criticism section because only you can evaluate this condition and apply reason to it. When you think that no one of importance loves or cares about you, your first investigation is to discover the reason associated to this lack of concern. When the typical group of people who are concerned for your well-being are gone from your circle of influence, no one else has any obligation to love you. Even if they did, you have no control over their reason for loving you or the amount of love that they display for you. And because this is out of your control, you should not allow their feelings to impact how you feel about yourself. The rebuttal to this assessment is that everybody needs love and you have it. To most people searching for love, the love that is available holds minimal significance to them. The love of God is always present and directed at everyone. **John 3:16 For God so loved the world, that he gave his only begotten Son, that whosoever believeth in him should not perish, but have everlasting life.** Outside of the love of God, any other love that you receive is optional. There used to be a strong belief that a mother's love was automatic and consistent; however, in today's society some children are without a mother's love, sometimes self-imposed and sometimes because of circumstance. If a mother's love is not guaranteed the others are subjective too. And because so many people link love and like together, if they don't like you it is quite possible and likely that they don't love you either. So you could be seeking something that is completely out of reach. This is one reason why it is so important that you love yourself.

To further understand being your toughest critic, you must find a way to always respect yourself. The Funk and

Wagnall's dictionary defines respect as follows: Respect is to have differential regard for; esteem. Respect is to treat with propriety or consideration. Respect is to regard as inviolable; to avoid intruding upon. Along with this definition comes an air of honor and dignity. To have self-respect requires a certain amount of work or effort and extreme discipline. Your attitude and demeanor will display that you respect yourself and cause you to demand that others respect you also. This behavior portrays that you expect to receive what you give. This respect for self requires that you establish a baseline of your expectations for yourself and for others toward you. It requires that you carry yourself in a specific manner and that you maintain that posture at all times. Others will respect you just because you maintain that level of discipline in your life. They won't have to wonder if you love yourself because they will be so taken by your respect for yourself. It is a myth that indicates that you have to take what people give you; if they choose not to respect you, your options are many. You could find a new circle of friends. You could demand that they don't label you in such terms anymore. Or, you could give them the right manner to address or treat you. Many will find reason to be offended by your newfound respect for yourself but most of the time they will honor your demands. As you think about it, the same rules apply to your own opinion of you.

Conceptual Summary

1. Acknowledgment that an event or behavior has occurred does not necessarily indicate responsibility for that event or behavior. However, acknowledgment of such activity allows one to address the issue and implement an action plan of resolution.

2. Assigning or shifting guilt and/or blame is only satisfying to the entity that is doing the assigning or shifting of that guilt or blame. Having the blame assigned can facilitate moving on to the next stage of resolution, such as forgiveness, root cause analysis, etc.

3. Criticism requires thought, but the recipient is the only one responsible for initiating any action or response. Reaction to the criticism may appease the contributor, but the contributor only makes the

statement and does not necessarily have any owner-ship in the criticism.

4. When you are your own critic, the judgment can be harsher than from other critics because you have an inside track on the capabilities of the recipient. Taking that information into consideration, you must have patience with yourself in order to avoid unnecessary stress.

5. Respect for yourself can easily be translated into love for yourself. Whether you acknowledge this fact internally others will observe it as fact.

Thought Provoking Queries

1. Do you have the ability to acknowledge and accept that an occurrence has happened without seeking to assign blame, fault, or responsibility to it?

2. Does assigning blame, guilt, or responsibility to an occurrence make you feel better about that occur-rence? Are you aware that blame assignment does nothing to the problem or issue?

3. Can you separate constructive criticism from being blamed for an occurrence?

4. Do you take constructive criticism as a personal attack on your performance or character?

5. Do you expect more of yourself than you expect of others? Does this make the issue a higher priority or do you feel that you are somehow better than your peers?

6. Do you respect yourself? How do you justify your answer to this question?

Chapter Fifteen

The Toughest Judge

S adly, you are your toughest critic. You probably don't know it but you often judge yourself far more harshly than anyone else would ever critique you. You observe and measure yourself up to standards that others may not even care about in someone else. This can cause you to find reason to dislike and to not love yourself. Usually this occurs when you are trying to measure up to some role model, mentor, or highly respected person. Something to consider here is that if God had wanted two of them He is more than capable of making another one, which does not have to be you. Another thought is that clones are never as good as the original. So if you are trying to be like someone other than Jesus Christ, you can only measure up so far and then consider that you are merely a substitute for the original. Meanwhile, we strive to be like Jesus because He is our perfect example. Knowing that He is perfect and we are not keeps the challenge before us with hope eternal. For all other models, we must realize that God made us to be who He wanted us to be. If adjustments are required, God has the power to implement them so that you remain His pleasurable model. **Jeremiah 18:2 Arise, and go down to the potter's house, and there I will cause thee to hear my words. 3 Then I went down to the potter's house, and, behold, he wrought a work on the wheels. 4 And the vessel that he made of clay was marred in the hand of the potter: so he made it again another vessel, as seemed good to the potter to make it. 5 Then the word of the LORD came to me, saying, 6 O house of Israel, cannot I do with you as this potter? saith the LORD. Behold, as the clay is in the potter's hand, so are ye in mine hand, O house of Israel.** When you consider that you belong to God and you have given Him permission to make you into whatever He chooses, you may learn that you are ever changing. The best perspective of this concept is that when we have tried to enhance, upgrade, and improve ourselves as much as we are able to, we still have the awesome excellence of our God to finish the job. As to being our toughest critic, we seldom have enough answers about our character, our limitations, God's expectations, and our goals to really make an informed assessment about who we really are. So we must learn to love the person that we know today. Tomorrow we may discover that we have had a hidden trait that surfaced before we can really understand what happened. God is still working on you until perfection. **Hebrews 13:20 Now the God of peace, that brought again from the dead our Lord Jesus, that great shepherd of the sheep, through the blood of the everlasting covenant, 21 Make you perfect in every good work to do his will, working in you that which is well-pleasing in his sight, through Jesus Christ; to whom be glory for ever and ever. Amen.** The conditions of life may force you to see that you are not the same person that you were in times past. This causes self-evaluation on a regular basis and a checking to understand what happened. But just like you were not a mature Christian when you received Christ, you are still developing in your physical life also. You must learn to accept who you are and to love who you are. This does not necessarily mean that you will like who you are during this observation. You may have to separate the concept of like and love so that you can develop the quality most needed at the time. Considering who you used to be and what you are today can be traumatic because of the changes. Some of us had physical prowess, captivating beauty, or notable abilities that are no longer active features in our present character. Be glad that you had something to remember and adjust to the new legacy. Don't try to recreate the past because you may find disappointment, increased lack of confidence, unanswered questions, and self-pity.

You are expected to evaluate yourself according to scripture, specifically concerning your faith in God. **II Corinthians 13:5 Examine yourselves, whether ye be in the faith; prove your own selves. Know ye not your own selves, how that Jesus Christ is in you, except ye be reprobates?** This scripture provides a pattern for us to examine our other characteristics and traits. Self-evaluation, when you are doing well or when you are performing as expected, can be gratifying. It still leaves room for analysis and improvement, if needed. However, even a good grade does not necessarily make you love yourself. When you are not achieving or producing according to your own expectations, you can begin to wallow in self-pity and even become depressed. Or when you feel that circumstances are forever going in the favor of others, you can develop a negative attitude about yourself and about life. These feelings can be magnified when you have a great concern about what others may see or think. The direct impact to you is that you have evaluated life and your place in it and have determined that you are not getting your fair share of the good, or you are receiving more than your fair share of the bad. In life, there is an expectation of having some days that are painted like this for all of us, but it is our responsibility to seek to overcome those days through contact with our God. As a statement of fact, the real reason to examine yourself is so that you can please your Lord and Master. This is of utmost importance. All other concerns should be secondary. Matters become even worse when you worry about the circumstances or what you can or cannot do about them. Yes, you are your own responsibility, so if you plan to do something about the critiqued issue, pray.

As you examine yourself, you must realize that only you are responsible for your perspective and your perception concerning your life. People and environment can influence events, but you have control over how you feel about yourself in those things. **Philippians 4:11 Not that I speak in respect of want: for I have learned, in whatsoever state I am, therewith to be content. 12 I know both how to be abased, and I know how to abound: every where and in all things I am instructed both to be full and to be hungry, both to abound and to suffer need. 13 I can do all things through Christ which strengtheneth me.** It is apparent that Paul didn't start out with this feeling and attitude of contentment. He wasn't just blessed with a gift of contentment. He had to learn to look at the situation, determine what he could or couldn't control. He had to find the portion of the events that dictated that the glass was half full instead of somehow only seeing that it was half empty. And then when he had assessed that things were completely out of his control, he still had hope because God can do anything. Mood swings, alleged bad days, the blues, chemical imbalances, etc. are labels that we give to unpleasant circumstances. They shouldn't last forever, and you should still love yourself in the midst of them. When they are prolonged, they become known as depression. And depression requires that you be delivered or healed by God strengthening you.

You must never glorify the negative or bad assessment of yourself. Bragging about how poor you are or were is not on the path to reformation. Making comparisons with others to assess who was in the worse situation only glorifies the bad situation. Putting the bad situation in the limelight should only be done when it is necessary to define recovery, to get prayer, or to show how God has delivered you in order to be used as part of your testimony. You should not use your circumstance to obtain attention, notoriety, or a moment of fame because you may become addicted to the attention and then begin to wallow in that pity. This will make it appear that you enjoy your suffering. You tend to talk about it rather than trying to overcome it, and seem to find satisfaction in allowing others to share your pain. The idea of attention for those who love themselves is that their audience doesn't just sit and hold hands as they absorb the sad story. On the contrary, the story is told to offer some advice, help, or prayer so that others can change their situations. Stories of negative experiences should give instruction, assistance, or a prayer; otherwise there is no reason to share the story. Most are not looking for another negative assessment; they've already have done that. Listeners are not looking for pity from another source; it merely implies that you have some idea of superiority and a false sense of being better. We are not here to glorify the negative circumstance because I do love myself.

Worrying about the evaluation and assessment of yourself, your circumstances, and your situation is only a way to expend energy, accomplish nothing good, and increase your stress. Evaluating the situation is different from worrying about it. Worrying about it is usually a predetermined state where you have decided that your situation is beyond your control, but you are still trying to determine if anything can be done. Evaluation of the circumstance is determining what is wrong and planning a strategy or a process to recovery. Worry does not necessarily involve anything past the effort that it takes to think about what has happened and how bad it is. You can tell by that statement that worry is not part of the solution. And the stress involved can cause you to dislike or hate yourself. You probably didn't realize that self-assessment can cause you to worry, but it can if you are not willing to do something about your circumstance.

Conceptual Summary

1. Since God sanctioned the union of your parents to create you, trying to be something that God did not make can be an exercise in futility. You will have to work with what you have within the capabilities of the product, with the limitations of its wisdom, and with the given time parameters.

2. To be unhappy with who you are is to indicate that God somehow made a mistake in either judgment or performance. Contrary to your opinion, God indicated that His work is good.

3. Since modifications to the end product will only make it a lesser product, you must adjust your opinions so that you can love what you have.

4. You may not notice the changes that time has developed in you, but God really isn't finished with you yet. Whether you believe yourself to be perfect or not, the result of God's efforts concerning you will be perfection.

5. The vanity of being pleased with yourself has its place, but to please your creator, lord, and master is more rewarding. Criticizing behavior and character results in wasted effort, if it doesn't contribute to purpose.

6. Avoid glorifying the negative qualities in yourself. It may produce empathy and sympathy in some, but ultimately you will only feel worse.

7. You are in control of how you feel about yourself. Others may influence environment and conditions surrounding you but only you control your perspective and your perception of yourself.

8. Don't set the standard for your performance, character, and accomplishment so high that it can never be reached without divine intervention. You will have enough failures to revisit without such lofty aspirations.

Thought Provoking Queries

1. Considering the characteristics that God put in you, are you be satisfied with God's work on you?

2. Are you content with whom you are? If not, why? If so, why?

3. Do the qualities that you do not care for in yourself warrant enough attention to be changed? Why do you feel so?

4. Are you sure that you would be more pleased with a different you?

5. Can you limit the amount of self-criticism to the amount that you would provide to others?

Chapter Sixteen

Time To Think About It

W hen you are attempting to implement or enact love for yourself, you will discover that there are enormous amounts of effort and thought to be exerted. The unpopular choice may often be the best direction to take in order to impose the best benefit or love for yourself. Since it may be unpopular, you may have apprehensions about following that path as the decision is being made but later you will find that you rejoice at making the right choice. This is exercising love for yourself. Taking an apathetic approach or just allowing life to happen will result in conclusions which typically indicate that you don't care about yourself. Accepting the easy way out or the convenient path may cause discontent or efforts to second guess your station in the long run. Despite taking the easy path, the responsibility for whatever occurs without your input will remain in your court until addressed. Laziness or less work does not equate to love for self. So taking control and accepting responsibility for internal affection is the only way to prove to yourself that you love yourself. The influence of others can impact how you feel about yourself if you give them that privilege. But no one can actually get inside you and determine what you really know and feel about yourself. So you must consider the tools and attributes that you were blessed with from birth and find contentment with them. Learn to utilize them as an advantage and develop a love for the skills and personality that you possess. No one else can do this for you. They can only provide temporary feelings of external affection while they are present, but you live with yourself indefinitely. Find a way to do the right thing for the person that you cannot escape – you. If you can understand yourself enough to love what God has given you, the objective of loving your neighbor will be much easier to accomplish.

When you love and respect yourself, there is always one person on earth in your corner. Even those closest to you may not understand the kind of love you require. To allow anyone besides God to influence how you feel about yourself is an act of enslavement or bondage. You shouldn't have to deal with this. Be willing to accept external love and its limitations with the understanding that if there is no other love available, you still have love for yourself. The scripture indicates that the example for loving others is to know how to love yourself. If this is not something that you truly understand, examine your personal feelings about each scenario, event, or circumstance. Understand what you would desire to occur for your benefit. Implement as much of that behavior as possible. Weigh the long term and the short term pros and cons. Apply God's will and what will benefit you best. Hopefully they coincide, but if they don't, talk to God about it. As you apply all of the concepts to yourself you will find that you look at others differently. This is not an accident.

CPSIA information can be obtained at www.ICGtesting.com
Printed in the USA
241220LV00003B/3/P

9 781613 796986